Contents at a Glance

Contents

Career Exploration Information   63

Finding and Applying for Job Openings   83

Career Clearinghouses   109

Researching Employer and Labor Market Information   *117*

Military Careers   *129*

Self-Employment and Small Business   *147*

Temporary, Freelance, Telecommuting, and Volunteer Work   165

About This Book

Our educational and job choices affect our lives profoundly, because we all seek a career path that supports us both personally and financially. Although some of us come out of school fixed on a particular career and others shift gears several times over a working lifetime, we all look for the same sort of satisfaction from our work.

As you embark on your career or prepare to change careers, you need to ask yourself a number of questions:

→ What education or training do I need to get the career I want?

→ How do I decide on the career—and employer—that is right for me?

→ How do I decide on the school or lifelong learning opportunities that are right for me?

→ How do I pay for my education?

→ Where do I investigate other options, such as the military, freelancing, or starting my own business?

The Web sites in this book have been carefully chosen to help you answer these questions, giving you the tools and information you need to take control of your educational and career path. Skip to the sections that apply to you and your individual goals, and explore the different choices available. There's a wide world of information out there, and it's up to you to take advantage of it!

—Rachel Singer Gordon

Internet Tips and Electronic Resumes

The Internet offers an unprecedented wealth of information to help you make informed decisions about your path in life. From choosing (and getting into) a college and finding financial aid to learning about careers, finding job openings, and investigating other options such as the military or self-employment, it's all online—if you can find it!

Because the online world presents so many opportunities, it can sometimes be hard to figure out the best places to begin out of the thousands of options available. That's why we've put together the very best career and education Web sites—nothing more, nothing less—to let you use the Internet as a powerful tool in your career and education decisions.

We've done the research for you and picked out the 400 or so sites that let you find the information you need quickly and easily. Of course, if you want to investigate further, we give you ideas for doing that, too. Not only do we talk about searching for additional career and education information online, we also point out when a Web site can lead you to further information and to other related sites. Look at these as the best way to get started on your quest for information and as one of the best ways to get (most) content free of charge.

Before we get started describing our sites, we'll tell you a little about finding and using information on the Internet, as well as how to create and use an electronic resume during your career explorations. Realize first that "the Internet" is basically just a giant network of computers, all connected to allow people to communicate and to share and find information. The most common ways people use the Internet—and the ones we'll talk about in this book—include the following:

→ **The World Wide Web (WWW or "the Web").** The Web lets you access information on Web sites, which can include text, pictures, video, audio, and more. Most of the Internet resources discussed in this book are Web sites.

→ **Electronic mail ("e-mail").** E-mail lets you send written messages to friends, relatives, and potential employers and lets them easily reply to you. Your messages can make it across the building or across the ocean within minutes—or even seconds. You can also send your resume and apply for jobs via e-mail. We'll talk more about that in the "Using Electronic Resumes" section later in this Introduction.

The World Wide Web

The World Wide Web is most often accessed through a piece of software called a Web browser, usually Internet Explorer or Netscape Navigator. (If you use an online service such as AOL, you also have the option of using its built-in Web browser, but Web sites look and behave basically the same way.) Each lets you navigate the Web through a graphical user interface, using your mouse to point and click your way to the information you need.

The point-and-click nature of the Web works because of the use of *hypertext*. Hypertext documents on the Web contain *hyperlinks* (or *links*), which connect you to other related information. When you click a word, phrase, button, or image that contains a link, a new Web page comes up on your screen. You can then choose to continue along that line of information, go back to your original location, or link off in yet another direction. Hypertext is what makes the sites in this book so useful, because each page links to yet more articles, information, and options!

Forget Something?

Never again. Not only can you now keep your calendar and schedule handily available on the Web, many places will e-mail you reminders before important events (such as a job interview!). It's like having your own virtual piece of string to tie around your finger.

If you sign up for a free e-mail account at a place like Hotmail.com or Yahoo!, calendaring comes with the service. All you have to do is remember to enter your appointments on the calendar.

Web Addresses

Web addresses (sometimes called URLs, or uniform resource locators) point you to specific Web sites on the Internet. A Web address works just like a postal address, identifying where on the Internet that particular Web site "lives." Although these addresses at first glance look somewhat confusing, there is a certain logic to them. We'll take an address apart and examine it piece by piece to show how it is put together.

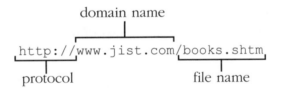

The beginning of any Internet address is the *protocol,* which tells the computer which part of the Internet you're using. For Web sites, you almost always see **http://**, which stands for Hypertext Transfer Protocol. Luckily, you don't need to type this part of the URL into a newer Web browser—it just assumes it's there.

www, which stands for World Wide Web, is often part of a Web address. Sometimes people leave it off when they talk about Web addresses (saying "jist.com" instead of "www.jist.com," for example). Just be aware that some URLs do not contain the www, and others get finicky if you leave it out. Also, variations are starting to pop up, such as "www2." Just type the Web address exactly as it appears and you will be fine.

jist.com is the domain name. It's basically the most important part of the Internet address, which gets you to the company, organization, or other entity that owns that domain. The part before the dot often is similar to the name of the company or other entity that owns the Web site. (In this case, "jist" stands for JIST Publishing.) The letters after the dot (the *extension*) identify what type of organization it is. Here are the most common extensions:

.com	for a commercial site
.biz	for companies
.edu	for a university or educational institution
.gov	for a government agency
.net	for a network
.org	for an association or organization
.mil	for a branch of the U.S. military
.info	for an informational site
.name	for individuals

To see all the different domain extensions, visit ICANN at www.icann.org. New extensions are being added to allow the Internet to continue to grow and develop, especially since the .com extension has become so overloaded. You can follow the discussions and arguments about when and why to add them at ICANN's Web site. Also note that you might run into even more extensions during your online travels. For example, each country is assigned a two-letter code. (The U.S. has been assigned .us, but most U.S. Web sites prefer to use .com, .org, or .edu.)

books.shtm is the file name of the information you're viewing—the name of that file on the computer you are visiting on the Internet. The last part of the file name is usually "htm," "html," or "shtm." (Sometimes you see newer file names that end in .asp or another group of letters, but just type them in exactly as you see them.) htm or html means Hypertext Markup Language, the language of the Web; an shtml file is just an html file that uses a slightly different technology. As with word-processing or spreadsheet files, you can copy, print, or save an htm, html, or shtml file.

Those are the basics of Web addresses! Of course, they can be much longer than our example. You often see directory paths between the domain name and file name, located between slashes. Directory paths just tell the host computer where to look for the file you want. A Web address can also specify a location within a file (a section further down the page, for example) or show the results of search criteria you've entered.

Searching the Web

Search engines and directories are special Web sites that have indexed large portions of the Internet. They allow you to specify the type of information you are looking for, and then they bring up a list of Web sites that meet your criteria. Although Web browsers such as Netscape Navigator and Internet Explorer include a Search option on their toolbar, there are many other ways to search as well. You can type the address of any search engine into your browser, just as you would visit any other Web site. We'll talk about some of your options next. If you find a search engine or directory you especially like, be sure to bookmark it or place it in your Favorites for easy one-click access.

The Power of Portals

Some people like setting a favorite search engine as their browser's home page so that they can quickly start looking for the information they need every time they go online. Because many search engines and directories have also transformed into *portals* that let you view your local news, weather, e-mail, and more on the same page you search from, setting one to be your home page just makes sense!

Search-engine portals can be powerful, time-saving tools in your job search. From a single Web site, they allow you to do the following:

- Get a free e-mail address. You can use this address just for your job search, to keep your personal and business correspondence separate.
- Locate employer contact information through links to online white pages and yellow pages.
- Find your way to an interview. Use the mapping feature on some portal pages (such as Yahoo!) to map the route from your house to the interview and then print it for take-along convenience.
- Stay informed. You can personalize your portal and have it deliver news, stock reports, and more based on the demographic data and preferences you provide when you register.
- Network by chatting with fellow job seekers and people employed in your field.
- Prepare for the inevitable job interview small talk by reading late-breaking headlines right on your search-engine page.
- Plan your relaxation time between interviews by reviewing local cable-TV listings and movie show times.
- Figure out how to dress for tomorrow's interview (and how much time to allow to get there) by checking the local weather forecast.

But first, let's talk about the basics of successful Internet searching. The first step in this process is to identify a topic you want to research. Different search engines can be better for different types of topics, or for broader as opposed to very specific searches, so your topic can influence the search engine you use. We'll talk more about different types of search engines and directories and when to use each in the next sections.

As soon as you have a topic in mind, you need to think about the best way to communicate that topic to a search engine. Computers are wonderful inventions, but they need help from you to do their job. When you know how to state your question in a way a search engine understands, you'll be much more likely to get back information that is useful to you.

Many search engines provide their visitors with help in searching, ranging from tutorials to sample searches; become an expert searcher by checking out some online tutorials. (See the section "More Options" for some places to start.)

There are two main varieties of search engine: indexed search engines and Internet directories. Some, however, combine both types on the same site for extra searching power, and some have morphed themselves into multifeatured personalized portal sites. (See the preceding sidebar, "The Power of Portals.") An indexed search engine might also partner with a directory (and vice versa) to provide both sophisticated Web access and a well-organized directory of sites.

When considering which type of search engine to use, consider what you're looking for. Directories are handy for exploring a general concept or broad, open-ended questions. Clicking through a list of categories might alert you to related topics you hadn't previously considered. Indexed search engines are best for finding a large variety of information on a specific or more narrowly defined topic.

Internet Directories

Internet directories use human reviewers to organize Web sites into categories that let visitors drill down from broad to very specific topics. For example, let's say you wanted to use Yahoo!, the best-known Internet directory, to get a list of sites that provide information on the federal minimum-wage law. You could drill down through the categories as follows: Business and Economy: Employment and Work: Employment and

The Challenge of Finding "The Right Stuff"

With all these search-engine options and all the information out there, it should be easy to find "the right stuff" online—right? Unfortunately, the sheer volume of information can make finding just the bit you want more challenging than ever. Although no one is sure of the exact size of the Web (and it gets bigger every day!), estimates range from 3 to 7 **billion** pages.

No one search engine can index all the Web sites, and each uses different methods, so a search in one engine might come up with very different results than a search in another. Sites such as Search Engine Showdown (described in the section "More Options") can give you an idea of the relative sizes and features of different search engines. In 2002, Google alone claimed to cover more than 3 billion Web pages—and even it doesn't index the whole Web.

The moral of the story is that if you find what you're looking for on the first try, great. If not, try another search engine, or another, or another.

Workplace Issues: Minimum Wage. Directories usually aim to provide just the "best" sites in each category, rather than creating a comprehensive index of as many Web sites as possible.

Many Internet directories also give you the option of doing a keyword search, but beware: They might be searching just their own directories and not the entire Web. Or, if they do include the rest of the Web in their search, their directory sites might get top billing over other Web sites. How do you know? Sometimes they tell you, but for the behind-the-scenes story, visit the Search Engine Showdown Web site, described later in this Introduction.

Here are some examples of Internet directories:

Open Directory Project

`http://dmoz.org`

The Netscape-administered Open Directory Project (ODP), the largest human-edited Web directory, is maintained entirely by volunteer editors. Editors are responsible for selecting, organizing, updating, and annotating the links in their own category. (Are you an expert on a subject? Consider signing up to help!) Unlike some other directories, ODP never charges to list URLs, but the quality of different categories can be inconsistent. Several major search engines use ODP data to power their own directories. ODP's motto? Humans do it better!

Yahoo!

www.yahoo.com

The most famous Internet directory, Yahoo! has transformed itself from a searchable directory to a full-featured Internet portal while retaining its core collection of categorized links. Search or drill down through its categories, or personalize your own Yahoo! home page to include access to e-mail, an appointment calendar, local weather, headline news, local TV listings and movie show times, your stock portfolio, and more! Click Help for search tips and other information on using and personalizing the site.

Indexed Search Engines

Indexed search engines vary tremendously in what they cover and how they categorize sites, but each uses computerized indexing rather than humans to index Web sites and then allows visitors to search through that index for information of interest.

To understand why you receive different results from each search engine, realize that some search engines index the entire contents of a Web page. Others index only specific parts, such as the title or top heading, or hone in on keywords that the Web page author embeds at the top of the page (inside a *meta-tag*) to describe that page's content. For example, some of the keywords for jist.com are resumes, job search, career, jobs, books, videos, reference, workbooks, assessments, and cover letters. Each applies to the types of material JIST publishes.

Each search engine also uses different criteria to rank Web sites, so one of the top sites to show up in one search engine might appear far down the list—or not at all—in another. These rankings can depend on how often your keyword appears on a particular Web page, how popular that page is (for example, how often it is linked from other Web sites), or a number of other factors.

Keyword searches are common, and you'll find them not only at search engines, but also within many Web sites. Many of the job banks described in chapter 4, for example, offer a keyword search to help you sort through their job listings.

Not only do search engines index the Internet differently, but each displays your results in different ways. Some, for example, show you the total number of pages found. Some display just the titles of the pages, and others provide annotations from their partner directory or descriptions provided by the Web page creators themselves.

Many search engines offer you the choice of doing simple or advanced searches. An advanced search usually gives you more control. A good plan is to try a simple search first and see what happens and then switch to an advanced search if you are unhappy with your initial results.

Here are some examples of indexed search engines:

AltaVista

www.altavista.com

> Through its "Prisma" service, AltaVista lets users refine their searches by suggesting related terms to search for. Sponsored links appear at the top of each list of results; scroll down the screen to see where the best matches to your query actually start. You can also switch to the directory (from LookSmart) to browse through categories rather than do a keyword search. AltaVista now charges for "express" inclusion in its database, but it also lists sites more slowly for free.

FAST

www.alltheweb.com

> FAST (also known as AlltheWeb) competes with Google (described next), each trying to outdo the other in indexing the largest number of Web sites. In late 2002, FAST claimed more than 2 billion fully indexed pages. It also covers more types of files than most other search engines and can search Flash and .pdf files as well as regular Web pages. FAST's advanced search provides a huge variety of options. Simple search has a handy check box to search for your terms as a phrase. Results show an excerpt from the actual site, with your search terms highlighted; sponsored links appear at the top of the list. Good, fast searching and uncluttered pages make FAST a winner in the search-engine wars.

Google

`www.google.com`

> Google's sense of humor is apparent in its name (a "googol" is a 1 followed by 100 zeroes), and in its penchant for decorating its logo to celebrate holidays and special occasions. In late 2002, Google claimed to search more than 3 billion Web pages, and it does so quickly and without overwhelming viewers with ads or other services. Sponsored links are clearly marked at the top and sides of results lists, and results highlight your search terms in an excerpt from that page. Google also offers special searches for news, different file types, and a large number of advanced search options. It uses Open Directory as its partner directory. Google offers a downloadable toolbar for Internet Explorer so that you can do an instant Google search at any time without first going to the Google home page.

Teoma

`www.teoma.com`

> A newer contender in the search-engine wars, Teoma also offers an Internet Explorer downloadable toolbar for easy searching. Search includes a check box to search for your terms as a phrase, and search results are divided into three sections: Results, Refine, and Resources. Results lists the Web page results, Refine gives ideas for refining your search, and Resources lists related collections of links. Sponsored links appear at the top. Teoma is owned by Ask Jeeves (described in the following section).

More Options

You didn't really think that indexed search engines and directories represent all your options in the wide world of Internet searching, did you? Your other choices here usually allow you to go bigger (with meta-search engines that search a number of search engines at once) or smaller (with subject-specific or specialized databases). Meta-search engines can save you time by searching a number of places at once, but it's harder to do an advanced search, because you don't have access to each site's tools.

Smaller or subject-specific databases can let you do a more focused search when you need a very specific piece of information, such as a phone number. The Web has hundreds of search engines. To find more, try exploring the sites listed in the next section, or check out the Internet Search Engine database at www.isedb.com.

Ask Jeeves

www.aj.com

Ask Jeeves aims to make searching simple by allowing searchers to ask questions rather than worry about formulating useful keywords (although you can still use keywords if you'd like). Ask Jeeves lists questions from its database that it thinks match your query at the top of its results, and you can click each to see its "answer." Or you can scroll down (through sponsored results and then to actual search results) for a more typical list of links. Jeeves also provides other related phrases to try your search on.

Dogpile

www.dogpile.com

Dogpile's motto, "Unleash the power of meta-search!", sums up this site, one of the first and most useful meta-search engines. Its front page offers the option to search, browse a Web directory, or search white and yellow pages for addresses and phone numbers. Results are grouped by the search engine they came from; the top ten results from each are listed, and then users have the option to click through to each search engine for the full list. Ideas for related searches appear at the top and bottom of the results page; advanced search options let you specify which search engines to use and to search for keywords as "any," "all," or "phrase."

Vivísimo

http://vivisimo.com

Another meta-search engine, Vivísimo searches a number of search engines and provides results both in a typical top results list and in "clusters" of information. Clusters group results into several related subjects, and you can choose any cluster to see the actual sites found. Each result shows the search engine(s) it came from, and you can click Preview to see a snippet of the site without having to load the whole page and move away from your results list. Advanced search lets you specify which search engines to use and to use a number of advanced syntax options for more precise searching.

WhitePages.com

www.whitepages.com

At WhitePages.com, you can find a person, a phone number, an area code, a ZIP code, a toll-free number, maps, and more. It's an all-around handy little site. You can also do reverse searches, in which you enter a phone number and get an address. This can come in handy for those "blind" job ads.

Search Engine Showdown

www.notess.com/search/

Librarian Greg Notess provides this "users' guide to Web searching" to help you make the most out of your Internet searches. You'll find reviews of search engines, news, statistics, tutorials, feature comparisons, and more. Search Engine Showdown also compares and discusses the major Internet directories, news and phone number search engines, and other related sites. It's the place to start for information on all the major search engines.

The Spider's Apprentice

www.monash.com/spidap.html

The Spider's Apprentice is "a helpful guide to Web search engines." Find search strategies, learn how search engines work, get tips on doing more-effective searches, and check out the rankings and in-depth analysis of the top search engines. Find out how your favorite search site stacks up!

Web Search Strategies

http://home.sprintmail.com/~debflanagan/main.html

Need even more help? Check out Debbie Flanagan's Web Search Strategies. Just like it sounds, Web Search Strategies is an online tutorial that guides you step-by-step through conducting an effective Internet search. You'll learn about using search engines, subject directories, meta-search engines, and specialty databases. It includes in-depth instruction on searching the most popular search engines, as well as practice searches to get you started.

E-Mail

Electronic mail (e-mail) is the Internet's most popular feature—and for good reason! E-mail lets you stay in touch with everyone from friends to coworkers, sending messages nearly instantly across the office, across the street, or around the world.

E-mail is the most basic tool in your Internet job search. It's nearly impossible today to conduct an effective job search without e-mail, and it's impossible to do an effective Internet job search without having a handle on e-mail basics.

E-mail is important partially because it

→ Allows employers to contact you quickly and easily

→ Allows you to send your electronic resume to potential employers

→ Allows you to receive notifications from personal job search agents (for more on job search agents, see chapter 4)

→ Allows employers to see you as a technologically savvy applicant

→ Allows you to network online with others in your field

E-mail software comes bundled with computer operating systems (such as Outlook Express in Windows) as well as in the software for online services such as America Online (AOL). You'll need an account from an Internet Service Provider (ISP) to use the e-mail software that comes with your computer or to use other free or commercial e-mail software you buy or download. (The two most popular free e-mail programs are Eudora, available at www.eudora.com, and Pegasus Mail, available at www.pmail.com.) You will need information from your ISP to set up your e-mail software initially, but most will walk you through the process over the phone in just a couple minutes. You can also sign up for free Web-based e-mail service on a number of Internet sites.

E-Mail Addresses

E-mail addresses, like Web site addresses, provide a standard way of locating someone on the Internet. They are put together in a fairly straightforward manner that makes sense when you realize what each part of the e-mail address does. Let's take a typical e-mail address and look at each part of it.

`rachel@lisjobs.com`

The first part of an e-mail address (**rachel**) is the user name, which identifies someone's unique mailbox or account at her ISP. You can usually pick your own user name, but on big Web-based e-mail providers, or online services such as AOL, so many people are using e-mail that you might have to add numbers or letters to make your user name unique. (This is how people end up with e-mail addresses with user names like "joezzz" or "fred123.")

Every e-mail address includes the **@** symbol. This is how you know it is an e-mail address rather than a Web site or another Internet address.

The part after the @ sign is the domain name (**lisjobs.com**). Just like the domain portion of a Web site address, this lets you know the company or organization that the e-mail address is part of.

Free Web-Based E-Mail

In addition to free e-mail software packages such as Eudora and Pegasus mail, a number of companies and Web sites now offer free Web-based e-mail service.

So what's in it for them? These Internet companies provide you free e-mail in return for your demographic information, which is valuable to them and their advertisers. You'll get the service for free, but you'll have to look at ads every time you use your online e-mail box. Some even e-mail you advertising in addition to the banner ads and other advertisements you see on the Web pages you use to access your e-mail.

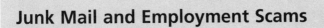

Junk Mail and Employment Scams

As you go through the Web sites listed in this book, you'll notice that a lot of them want your e-mail address. Some want to send you newsletters, some require an e-mail address when you register to use their site, and some need it to send you job openings that match your criteria.

Add all these messages to the "junk mail" that most Internet users receive, and messages from potential employers could get lost in the shuffle. (By the end of 2002, researchers estimated that more than 30 percent of all e-mail was unsolicited—a problem worse than those unwanted catalogs and credit-card offers piling up in your postal mailbox each day!)

To help cut through the clutter, why not take advantage of free Web-based e-mail services? Use free e-mail to be ultra-selective about who you give your "main" e-mail address to, or use a free address temporarily as a place to receive job notices.

Realize, too, that junk mail lives up to its name, and don't waste your time replying to people who send you unsolicited offers. Some unscrupulous companies target job seekers by junk-mailing them with offers of employment, home-based work, or resume services. These unsolicited scams cost job seekers huge amounts of time and money each year. Here are some tips to help keep you from being taken:

- Never send money, your Social Security number, credit-card information, or bank-account information to people who e-mail you unsolicited offers of employment.

- Don't bother signing up for offers from "resume-blasting" services that promise to send your resume to thousands of employers. Real employers delete resumes from these "services" unread, and your resume will end up annoying thousands of people who aren't hiring.

- No one makes thousands of dollars in their spare time by stuffing envelopes or assembling products at home. These are online versions of old scams.

- Check out companies with the Better Business Bureau if you are unsure about their legitimacy. You can do this online at http://search.bbb.org/search.html.

- Be wary of any unsolicited mail from "employment firms" that guarantee they will find you a job in return for your up-front payment.

Remember, if an offer sounds too good to be true, it probably is! Use your common sense to keep from being scammed, and check out the Riley Guide's Scams & Schemes page for more great tips and articles: www.rileyguide.com/scams.html.

So what's in it for you? Web-based e-mail services allow you to read and send e-mail from any Internet-connected computer—at the library, at home, at work, at school, or at a friend's house. It also provides you with a consistent e-mail address: Even if you change ISPs and lose your e-mail address with your provider, your Web-based address stays the same. If

Signature, Please!

Your e-mail signature is simply a little block of text that is automatically included at the bottom of each of your outgoing e-mail messages. This can include your name and contact information, a quote, a pitch, a tagline, or a message that sums up you and your qualifications.

Almost all e-mail software and Web-based e-mail allows you to create a signature. Why not make yours useful to employers and show your enthusiasm? A job seeker may try something like this:

> Looking forward to putting my five years of *(specific work experience)* to work for you.

Or:

> Member, *(name of job-related professional associations to which you belong)*

Put your contact information in your signature to make sure you don't forget to include it in the e-mail cover letters you send. Get creative if you want. Test it. But be sure to keep your signature brief and professional. Don't impose on readers by including huge quotes that are longer than your e-mail message itself, for example!

you share an Internet account with others in your family, you can use Web-based e-mail to set up a private e-mail address. Some of these e-mail providers also include calendars and other add-ons to make Web-based e-mail even-more useful.

You can use the Free Email Providers Guide at www.fepg.net to locate the Web mail that is right for you, or check out some of the sites in the next section.

Here are some examples of free Web-based e-mail providers:

Eudora Web Mail

www.eudoramail.com

> Eudora Web Mail, now part of Lycos, includes all the features you expect from Web-based e-mail, plus the ability to check your other e-mail accounts, all through your Eudora Web Mail box. This site also includes some nice junk-mail protection features and 5 megabytes of free storage space.

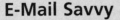

E-Mail Savvy

During your job search, you've probably spent a lot of time developing your network of contacts. Why spend time scrolling through hundreds of old e-mail messages trying to find someone's contact information or messages on a specific topic? Use the capabilities of your e-mail software or Web mail to get organized.

Common e-mail functions include

- Setting up mailboxes (or folders) to archive and organize old messages
- Saving and organizing e-mail addresses in an address book
- Saving the e-mail addresses of a group of people together, to easily send to the group without typing each individual address
- Sorting e-mails by status, priority, sender, date, subject, and so on
- Setting up filters to automatically direct incoming mail to a particular folder or mailbox
- Setting up filters to automatically open, copy, print, or delete a message

Taking a moment to read your program's manual or Help menu can save you time and help you organize your all-important e-mail. Now that's a win-win proposition!

Hotmail

www.hotmail.com

> Hotmail is the granddaddy of Web-based e-mail services. Part of the Microsoft Network, it provides 2 megabytes of free storage space, plus an address book, calendar, and other features. Unfortunately, it tends to attract a large amount of junk mail.

Yahoo! Mail

http://mail.yahoo.com

> Yahoo! Mail, part of Yahoo!'s portal services, includes a calendar, 4 megabytes of free storage, and other standard tools.

E-Mail Etiquette

→ Be brief.

→ Be professional. Avoid profanity, slang, and so on in any message to colleagues or a potential employer. If you wouldn't put it in a print cover letter, don't include it in your e-mail message, either.

→ Avoid using only capital letters. It's annoying to read, and it looks like shouting.

→ Be clear. People used to get excited about acronyms and emoticons (those sideways smiley or frowny faces made with punctuation marks), stemming from pre-Web days before color and graphic capabilities. It might be risky to assume that your reader understands—or will be amused by—IMHO (in my humble opinion), LOL (laughing out loud), or :). These are better used with friends than with potential employers.

→ Be selective. Send your message only to those who need to see it.

→ Check your spelling. Most e-mail software now includes spell-check features.

Using Electronic Resumes

Today, making an electronic resume is almost the same as making a regular resume. Have you typed your resume in Microsoft Word (or another word-processing program)? Have you saved it to a floppy disk or to your computer's hard drive? If so, your resume is already available in an electronic format—it's that easy! From there, the rest is simple. You just need to start with your Word resume and take a couple of steps to change it into other commonly requested formats. You're then ready to post it online or e-mail it directly to employers.

If you need help creating a resume, check out Susan Britton Whitcomb's *Résumé Magic* (JIST Publishing, 2003) or see the resume Web sites listed in chapter 4.

Types of Electronic Resumes

There are three common types of electronic resumes. This section explains how to create and when to use each.

→ **Microsoft Word.** You'll often see job ads requesting that candidates send their resume in "Word format." They are asking for a copy of the file you create when you type up and save your resume in Microsoft Word. If you use another word-processing program to create your resume, such as WordPerfect, don't worry. Almost all of them nowadays can save documents in Microsoft Word format. (Typically, all you have to do when saving your file is pick Save As… from the File menu. Then select Microsoft Word from the options listed.)

→ **ASCII (or "plain-text") resumes.** ASCII resumes are the lowest common denominator of electronic resumes. Although they might look plain and boring, some employers prefer to receive this type of resume to help them scan more easily for keywords and to reduce their risk of catching a computer virus from Word resumes. The easiest way to create an ASCII resume is to open your Microsoft Word resume and select Save As… from the File menu. Select Plain Text with Line Breaks from the options listed, and click Save. (Ignore any warnings Word gives you about losing formatting.)

Your resume is then saved as plain text. You can check by looking in the directory where you saved it. Your original resume will be listed as *resume name*.doc, and your text resume will be listed as *resume name*.txt.

Only one more step to go! Open your plain-text resume in a program such as Windows Notepad. Just double-click the name of the .txt file when you are looking at your directory. Notice that all the special formatting from your Word resume, such as bold, underline, and bullets, has been lost. You need to go through your text resume in Notepad and make it look as nice as possible without using any special formatting, because this is exactly how an employer will see your resume. When you're done, just resave it.

→ **HTML (or "Web page") resumes.** You can put your resume online in the form of a Web page. This allows you to do things such as include links from your resume to projects you have done, your e-mail address, and other useful information for employers. Putting your resume online as a Web page also allows employers to find you! This is easier than ever before because of cheap graphical Web page editing software such as Microsoft FrontPage and free Web hosting services such as Tripod.com. You can even use Microsoft Word to create a basic HTML resume by picking Save As... from the File menu and choosing HTML. Also check to see whether your school allows students to post resumes online, which might help employers find you from your school's Web site.

One of the things to be especially careful about with your Web page resume is to keep it looking as professional as possible. Because it is so easy to add pictures, music, and so on to a Web page, sometimes people go overboard and make employers look at family photos and listen to songs. You don't want to distract anyone looking at your HTML resume from its main point: you and your qualifications!

Using Keywords

You will want to use keywords to make your resume match employers' job ads as closely as possible. This is especially important if you are applying to large companies, which might use a computer to search through all the resumes it receives and reject any without the right keywords—before a human being even gets to look at them! No, it

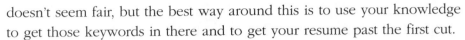

doesn't seem fair, but the best way around this is to use your knowledge to get those keywords in there and to get your resume past the first cut.

Luckily, you've already put your resume in electronic format, which means it's going to be really easy for you to make changes to it and get those keywords in there when responding to ads.

The main thing to realize when thinking about which keywords to put in your resume is that computers, although they let you do wonderful things (such as find career and education info online!), are just not very smart. They don't have the same power that people do to think and interpret. So your job here is to use keywords that give the computer exactly what it is looking for.

Let's say you see a job ad that asks for knowledge of Microsoft Access. You might have been working in an office for years and are familiar with Microsoft Access, Word, and all the other parts of the Microsoft Office software suite. The temptation is to just list "Microsoft Office" as a skill on your resume. The danger is that the computer might not know that Access is part of Microsoft Office and will toss out your resume. Therefore, if a job ad asks for a specific skill, use exactly the same words as in the job ad. Don't write "Microsoft Office." Instead, write "Microsoft Excel, Access, Word, and PowerPoint."

Always be as specific as possible. Read each job ad carefully, and be ready and willing to make changes to your resume when applying for different positions.

Getting Your Resume Online

There are a couple of different ways to get your resume online and in front of employers. The first, and easiest, is to respond to employers who ask for a copy of your Microsoft Word or plain-text resume via e-mail. (If you don't have an e-mail address yet, check out the section "Free Web-Based E-Mail" for ideas on how to get a free one.)

Employers who want a Word resume will want it as an e-mail attachment. Make sure that you know where your resume is saved on your floppy disk or hard drive and what you named it. Any e-mail software program lets you attach a file to a message. Just write a message including your cover letter, and then select the option in your software or in your Web mail to attach a file. Browse to the place you have saved your

Copy and Paste: Your Time-Saving Friends

Use your word processor's copy and paste functions when you need to copy the contents of your electronic resume into an e-mail message or online form. Just a few simple steps will get you squared away!

1. Open your plain-text resume in Notepad.

2. Choose Edit... Select All. The computer highlights your whole resume.

3. Choose Edit... Copy to place your resume in the computer's memory.

4. Click back over to your e-mail message or Web page.

5. Make sure the cursor is blinking inside the message or in your online form at the spot where you need to place your resume. If not, just click inside the message or form box.

6. Choose Edit... Paste.

That's it! You should now see your resume pasted into the message or form, just as it appeared in Notepad. You can also use handy keyboard shortcuts—Ctrl-A for Select All, Ctrl-C for Copy, and Ctrl-V for Paste. Use whichever way is easiest for you.

resume, and select that file to attach to your e-mail message. It will be sent with the message so that the employer can open it and see it just as you saved it.

Employers who specify a plain-text resume will want it either as an attachment or inside the e-mail message itself. If they want it inside the message, first type your cover letter as an e-mail to the employer. Then open your plain-text resume in Notepad and use copy and paste to include the text of your resume right under your cover letter.

The next way to get your resume online is to post it in a resume bank on one of the major job boards, such as Monster. (You'll find information on a bunch of these in chapter 4.) When you see the option to post your resume online, you usually get a form to fill out. Again, use copy and paste to put your plain-text resume into this form.

Using your resume electronically saves you and employers time, saves you from having to print and mail multiple copies, and shows potential employers that you have some computer know-how. Many of the Web pages in this book give you the opportunity to use your electronic resume, so have it ready to go. Take advantage of everything these sites have to offer!

CHAPTER 1

College and Financial Aid Information

Higher education brings a number of benefits, from career success and satisfaction to personal enhancement. Of all the advantages of getting a college education, though, the easiest to see is that of increased earning potential. To put it plainly, college graduates just tend to make more money.

Although the cost of a college education has been increasing, so has the gap between what college graduates earn as opposed to those with only a high school education. According to a 2002 U.S. Census Bureau report (called, appropriately, "The Big Payoff"), a college-educated full-time worker can expect to earn about $22,000 more annually than a high school graduate—or almost $1 million more over the course of a career!

Because getting into and through college can be a job in itself, it's lucky that there are a number of Web sites to help you get started with choosing the right college and funding your education. Save time and money by investigating your options online as you begin your adventures in higher education.

Researching Colleges

These Web sites are the best places to begin looking for information on specific schools. Some of these sites include more listings, so if you don't find what you're looking for at one of these sites, try another. Several also include information on financial aid, getting into schools, and much more, so spend some time browsing to see what is available.

CampusTours.com

www.campustours.com

"Virtual" college tours here range from straightforward online videos about a school to 360-degree panoramic images. Extras include maps, photos, webcams, and links to university Web sites. To take full advantage of CampusTours, make sure you have the latest versions of the Shockwave, RealPlayer, and QuickTime plug-ins—all of which can be downloaded and installed from this site. Take the opportunity to view what each campus has to offer without having to travel.

CollegeView

`www.collegeview.com`

Hobson's CollegeView lets you search for your ideal college by criteria such as area of study, location, student body size, public/private, and religious affiliation. You can then see facts, contact information, virtual tours, and Web sites for your selected school(s). Additional information includes feature articles and in-depth guides on topics such as Christian colleges and studying health and medicine, a comprehensive guide to finding and applying for financial aid, and a career-planning center aimed at college students.

CollegeXpress

`www.collegexpress.com`

Colleges, scholarships, and loans—oh my! CollegeXpress provides a handy way to request information from multiple schools. Just check off those you're interested in, and CollegeXpress forwards your request to the school. First, though, you have to complete the site's free registration form. You'll find information on schools; some have more in-depth profiles than others. Some even allow you to apply online. You can also read helpful articles or "Ask the Dean" your questions via the online message board. Of course, you can find financial aid information here as well.

Community College Web

`www.mcli.dist.maricopa.edu/cc/`

Community College Web is just that—a collection of links to almost 1,300 community college Web sites in the U.S., Canada, and around the world, as well as many links to other community college-related resources. Use the search form to find colleges' Web sites by name, location, or keyword. The site is maintained by the Maricopa Center for Learning and Instruction of the Maricopa Community Colleges system in Arizona.

Gradschools.com

`www.gradschools.com`

Gradschools.com concentrates on links to graduate programs— more than 53,000 of them in various areas of study nationwide.

Search by subject or by school, select your preferred geographic location, and you'll be presented with contact information and a Web link for each program. You can register to be recruited by schools in your area of interest and talk to other students online in chat rooms and discussion boards. You also can browse through the information center to find information on applying to and surviving grad school.

myFootpath.com

www.myfootpath.com

The folks at myFootpath.com call themselves the "experts in college admissions," and you'll find a lot of information on the process here. Read Q&A articles in the Ask the Counselor section, browse articles on college prep and college life, and sign up for a free e-mail newsletter. If you have a particular school in mind, you can also purchase inside admissions reports on specific colleges to get in-depth information on the application process.

Peterson's Education Portal

www.petersons.com

Although Peterson's is a company best known for its test-prep and admissions guides, it provides quite a bit of free information on this extensive site. Search for graduate programs, distance-learning programs, and undergraduate schools to get the facts, see contact information, and find ways to apply online, or visit the schools' own sites for further info. Register to get recruited by schools and for the BestCollegePicks college-matching service, which recommends the best schools for you based on your profile. You have to complete the free registration to find scholarship information.

The Princeton Review

www.princetonreview.com

In the fall of 2002, The Princeton Review combined with Embark.com to offer even more information on schools, admissions, financial aid, and testing. You'll find everything from college ranking information to articles on choosing and getting into a school. While visiting, also work on your test-taking skills with free online practice tests (SAT, ACT, and more), research colleges, and apply to selected schools online. Register to save your search and quiz results and to be recruited by schools. If you're daring, use the "tuition cost calculator" to estimate the true price of your education.

RateMyProfessors.com

www.ratemyprofessors.com

Here you can get tips on professors to select—or avoid. Check out the professors who are listed from the schools you are considering, and see what their students have to say about them. Each is rated on a 1-to-5 scale in several categories, with optional comments.

RWM Vocational School Database

www.rwm.org/rwm

Considering alternatives to a traditional college education? Visit the RWM Vocational School Database to browse its directory of vocational programs by state and occupation. All schools are state-licensed or accredited.

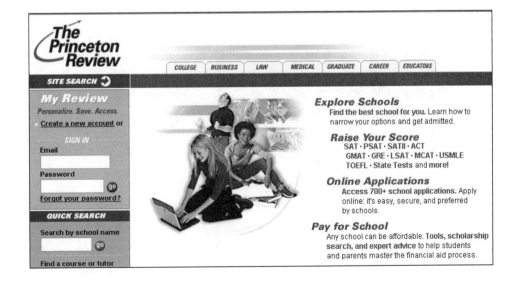

University Links

www.ulinks.com

Search for colleges and universities by traditional categories such as name, location, and area of study, or pick a major category (military schools, medical schools, Catholic schools) to browse lists of schools. A unique feature is the ability to browse through school-sponsored sites for student newspapers, libraries, and other college and university features.

U.S. Two-Year Colleges

www.cset.sp.utoledo.edu/twoyrcol.html

Like Community College Web, U.S. Two-Year colleges is a directory of sites and contact information. It is arranged by state; you can't search by the name of the school. It includes links to relevant state agencies as well as links to specific schools. If you don't find your school listed, try one of the other two-year college directories listed on this site. U.S. Two-Year Colleges is provided by Engineering Technology Computing in the College of Engineering at the University of Toledo (Ohio).

U.S. Universities

www.usuniversities.com

The meat of this site lies in its directories. The main U.S. Universities directory allows you to search by state and/or degree program. Each listing contains contact information, a description of the school, and a listing of its programs, as well as a link to e-mail the university for more information. The site also contains a useful section on studying abroad, which you can search by country and/or subject. The site also has separate directories for high school students interested in foreign programs and for overseas internships, volunteer and teaching opportunities, and overseas jobs.

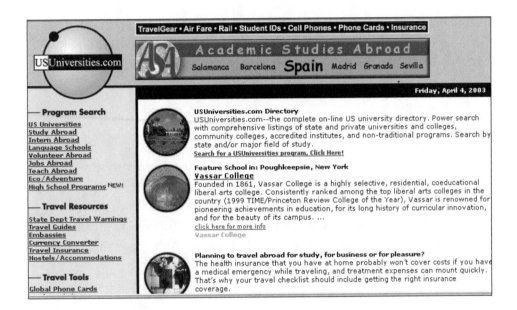

Web U.S. Higher Education

www.utexas.edu/world/univ/

This directory provides links to regionally accredited U.S. universities and community colleges. Browse by state, alphabetically, or through the What's New section to see recent additions. The site is sparse, but it requires no registration—and it shows you no ads!

Apply Online!

Many individual schools let you apply online, but the following sites let you complete common application information and reuse it for multiple applications—saving you time and typing.

CollegeNET

www.collegenet.com

Apply online to more than 1,500 colleges and universities. CollegeNET saves common information to save you time filling out forms. Search for the school or schools you want to apply to; read about tuition, contact information, deadlines, and admission requirements; and then choose your type of application. The custom search allows you to enter a number of customized criteria without having to register. Financial aid links and a scholarship search help you find funding after you apply.

Common Application

`www.commonapp.org`

The common application allows applicants to apply to any of 230 selective colleges and universities just by filling out one form. Complete the application online or download and print the form in .PDF (Adobe Acrobat; www.adobe.com) format. You can also find brief information on and a link to the Web site/e-mail address of any of the participating schools.

Getting the Scoop on College Entrance Exams

So you've finally narrowed it down to your top few choices—but don't forget that almost any school will require you to take one or more entrance exams. The following sites help you find out about common tests, register for them, and sign up for test-preparation courses online. Note that some sites mentioned earlier in this chapter, such as Peterson's Education Portal and The Princeton Review, are also good sources of testing information and resources.

ACT

`www.act.org`

The ACT assessment is one of the most commonly required examinations for college applicants. Here, you can find sample questions and information on registering for and taking the test, request scores online, and view answers to frequently asked questions. You might also want to check out the Information for Students section, which includes discussions of planning for college, choosing a career, and planning for the workplace.

College Board Online

www.collegeboard.com

> Register online for the SAT, PSAT, CLEP, and SAT II, or request your scores to be sent to schools. You can also take free diagnostic tests or purchase test-taking software and learn about what the different tests cover and how scores are calculated. Students with disabilities can also find out about requesting accommodations for certain tests. Additional information on this site helps you plan for college, choose a school, and find out about financial aid options.

ETS (Educational Testing Service) Net

www.ets.org

> Learn about popular tests such as the AP exams, the GRE, SAT I and II, and TOEFL at this Web site. (Note that some options link you back to College Board Online.) You can download demos of the online versions of several tests to see whether the computer-based testing option is right for you, or locate nearby test centers. ETS also guides you to free and low-cost test-preparation materials.

Kaplan

www.kaptest.com

> The name Kaplan is synonymous with test-preparation courses. At kaptest.com, you can find in-person courses near you or find free online practice questions and suggested strategies for success. Kaplan also sells in-depth online test-preparation courses that you can take when it's convenient for you. This is one of the best places to find information and tips on the various tests.

Your Money's Worth: College Rankings

U.S. News and World Report each year ranks the best colleges and graduate programs in a number of categories. A number of other magazines and Web sites have begun creating their own similar rankings. Although these are always somewhat subjective, rankings are a starting point to identify good schools to investigate further.

College and University Rankings (UIUC)

www.library.uiuc.edu/edx/rankings.htm

> The University of Illinois Urbana-Champaign provides a large list of categorized links to college rankings, from undergraduate institutions to law schools. Use this site to locate lists of wired colleges, those that are a best value, disability-friendly schools, and more. Also check out information on the validity of rankings and resources to investigate further.

USNews.com Education

www.usnews.com/usnews/edu/eduhome.htm

> Beyond the school rankings for which it is known, U.S. News provides all the other features you'd expect from an education Web site: news, articles, campus profiles, college search tools, financial aid guides, and calculators. You can also connect with others and get professional advice in the online forums, or sign up for free

e-mail newsletters in your area of interest. Information is helpfully divided by area: Choose from college, community college, graduate school, e-learning, or financial aid to access a wealth of articles, resources, tools, and rankings in each category. U.S. News explains how rankings are determined, how data is collected, and how best to use its lists, so be sure to read the explanations to help you make your own judgments.

Money Matters

Scholarships, loans, and savings plans are all important components in affording a college education. The following sites help you identify your financial aid options—and, if it's early enough, get started with saving! Many also include additional information on choosing, applying to, and getting through school, so it can be worth taking the time to explore what is available on each.

Adventures In Education

AdventuresinEducation.org

Sponsored by the Texas Guaranteed Student Loan Corporation, Adventures In Education provides information in English and Spanish for prospective college students—starting with a plan you can begin as early as middle school. Students, parents, and counselors can begin with the "tour guide" to get a step-by-step road map through the financial aid maze. Helpful worksheets, Internet links, and clear instructions help you choose and apply to school, pay for college, select a career path, and find a job after graduation.

College Is Possible

www.collegeispossible.org

The Coalition of America's Colleges and Universities launched the College Is Possible campaign in response to growing concern about the cost of a college education. The site's four major sections—on preparing for college, choosing the right college, paying for college, and adult students—help break the process into manageable chunks. Each section includes resources, tips, and straightforward information for current and aspiring students. As a noncommercial site, College Is Possible can be more forthcoming than some other resources about the true advantages and disadvantages of taking out loans and other ways of funding an education.

College Savings Plans Network

www.collegesavings.org

All 50 states now offer the 529 college savings plan (named after the part of the IRS code that authorizes them), and this site links to information on each state's unique programs. You'll find out about the 529 savings program, which allows families to put aside federal tax-exempt savings for college or purchase prepaid, locked-in tuition to state schools.

eStudentLoan.com

`http://apps.estudentloan.com/exec/loanfinder`

You need to register to use this free service, which allows you to search for both private and government loan programs. Follow the step-by-step guide to see what types of programs you qualify for, and then request applications or even apply online. eStudentLoan provides information on each loan, such as APR, fees, term, and average monthly payment, giving you the facts you need to make an informed decision.

FastWeb

`www.fastweb.com`

FastWeb is the place to start your search for college scholarships, but you need to complete the free registration form to conduct a search. Note that the extensive signup process includes a number of offers for magazine subscriptions and other unrelated information. Just pick "no, thank you" for each to avoid getting junk mail from these companies. FastWeb shows you information, requirements, and deadlines for each scholarship you potentially qualify for. Also try the school search for campus suggestions, or visit the Articles and Tools section for information and advice on financial aid and college/career planning.

Federal Student Financial Assistance

`www.ed.gov/offices/OSFAP/Students`

The federal government is one of the first places to turn for student aid, and this site from the Department of Education outlines the various programs that are offered. Explore your options with the "finding out about financial aid" guide, which describes loans, tax cuts, state aid, and aid from other federal agencies. You can also fill out the FAFSA (Free Application for Federal Student Aid) online. The section on completing the FAFSA walks you through the application and explains why certain questions are even asked. Because after you've taken out loans you have to worry about repaying them, the information here on repaying, consolidating, or finding forgiveness programs for existing loans is useful for graduates. (Be careful when typing the Web address for this site, because it is case-sensitive.)

FinAid!

`www.finaid.org`

Established in 1994, this award-winning site has grown into the most comprehensive online clearinghouse on funding a college education. Choose from loans, scholarships, military aid, or other types of aid to learn about all your options, and then check out extra tools such as links to financial aid applications, calculators, and personalized advice. Also sign up for a free monthly e-mail newsletter, and check out offers for free pamphlets and other financial aid resources.

FreSch! The Free Scholarship Search and Information Service

`www.freschinfo.com`

After being scammed by a fee-based scholarship search more than four years ago, Laura DiFiore started FreSch! to help other students avoid similar scams. Unlike other scholarship search sites, FreSch! does not require you to register before conducting a search. Her scholarship search includes more than 5,000 programs. You should also read the Scams section for advice on how to avoid being taken. Additional sections on selecting a college and other types of aid are useful but are less extensive than on other sites.

Mapping Your Future

`http://mapping-your-future.org`

Although Mapping Your Future provides information on the career-planning process, the main focus of this site is selecting and paying for college. The helpful guided tours lead you step-by-step through the process, and each includes a number of links to extra information. Special features include the ability to conduct loan counseling interviews online, financial fitness guides and calculators, scheduled interactive chat sessions on financial aid topics, and information on selecting and working toward a career. For more local information, check out the list of sponsors to see whether there is a link to an agency in your state.

Nellie Mae

www.nelliemae.com

 Nellie Mae, a wholly owned subsidiary of SLM Corporation (Sallie Mae, described next), allows you to apply or prequalify online for student loans. In many cases it provides an instantaneous response. You also can conduct loan entrance/exit interviews, check your loan status, or change your information, all at your convenience and all online. You'll learn about the different types of loans that are offered, including requirements, fees, interest rates, and repayment options. The EDvisor Debt Management section can help you keep track of your payments, especially if you take out multiple loans.

Sallie Mae: Student Loan Marketing Association

www.salliemae.com

Sallie Mae, the leading provider of education loans, primarily funds federally guaranteed student loans. If you're applying for federal aid, it's likely that at some point you'll be talking to the people at Sallie Mae. You can apply for or manage your loans online, read financial aid FAQs, and even make payments over the Web. The College Planning section walks you through the process of selecting, applying to, and paying for school, and the Wiredscholar section allows you to conduct a free scholarship search. (Wiredscholar is described at the end of this section.)

SmartMoney University

http://smartmoneyuniversity.com/Departments/CollegePlanning/

SmartMoney University provides online "courses" for parents to help them figure out how to pay for their children's education. It covers investing, savings plans, and strategies to avoid having a big chunk of your college savings go toward federal taxes. Worksheets, sample portfolios, stories, and straightforward advice make this a reassuring and commonsense guide for any family trying to save for college.

SRN (Scholarship Resource Network) Express

www.srnexpress.com

SRN Express includes more than 8,000 scholarship programs in a searchable database, as well as student loan forgiveness and consolidation programs for graduates seeking debt relief. You need to create a free profile in order to search.

Students.gov

www.students.gov

This site contains advice from the U.S. government on planning and paying for a college education, choosing a career, and planning a career in the military. Each section includes a number of links to more-specific information on each topic, and the database of sites is searchable. The Quick Connections menus link to sites outlining some of the most popular government services in each area.

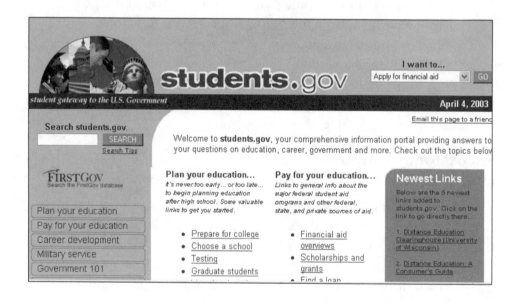

Upromise

www.upromise.com

✓ Start saving for college for yourself or your children by signing up with Upromise. Register your credit cards, grocery cards, and more to receive money back for college on the purchases you make. Upromise accounts can also be linked to a 529 savings plan (see the earlier review of the College Savings Plans Network).

wiredscholar

www.wiredscholar.com

✓ This Web site from Sallie Mae has step-by-step instructions for students (and parents), taking you through the college selection, application, decision, and financing process. A helpful chart allows you to compare features of various federal loan programs at a glance, and an online "award analyzer" lets you compare financial aid packages from each school that accepts you.

Interstate Student Exchange Programs

The following four organizations sponsor programs that allow students to pursue degrees (in specified majors) at out-of-state institutions at less than the normal out-of-state tuition. This can result in significant savings if you intend to attend school in another state. These programs also help reduce duplication of degree programs and help institutions with extra capacity fill their classes—a win-win situation.

Midwestern Higher Education Commission (MHEC) Midwest Student Exchange Program

www.mhec.org/resources_studentexchange.html

The Midwest Student Exchange Program of the Midwestern Higher Education Commission (MHEC) serves students from Kansas, Michigan, Minnesota, Missouri, Nebraska, and North Dakota. Read yearly bulletins and brochures outlining the program, available here in .PDF (Adobe Acrobat; www.adobe.com) format, to find out which institutions participate in the program, which degree programs are eligible for savings, how to apply, and the type of tuition breaks you might qualify for.

New England Board of Higher Education (NEBHE) Tuition Assistance

www.nebhe.org/explain.html

If you're a resident of Connecticut, Maine, Massachusetts, New Hampshire, Rhode Island, or Vermont, the New England Regional Student Program (RSP) might save you money. Sponsored by the New England Board of Higher Education (NEBHE), the RSP provides a tuition break for students to study certain majors (that are not available at public colleges in their own state) at public colleges and universities in other New England states. Majors at all levels of study and participating institutions are listed in each year's RSP catalog, which is available for browsing online. You also can find out about the program and average savings.

Southern Regional Education Board (SREB) Academic Common Market

www.sreb.org/programs/acm/acmindex.asp

Through the Southern Regional Education Board (SREB) Academic Common Market program, residents can pursue unique majors at regional public institutions outside their home states while paying in-state tuition. A new initiative allows students to take certain degree programs electronically from home at in-state rates. You also find out about the SREB Regional Contract Program, which gives out-of-state tuition breaks to students pursuing professional health degrees in fields such as dentistry and veterinary medicine. SREB's 16 member states are Alabama, Arkansas, Delaware, Florida, Georgia, Kentucky, Louisiana, Maryland, Mississippi, North Carolina, Oklahoma, South Carolina, Tennessee, Texas, Virginia, and West Virginia. This Web site includes information and contacts for specific programs in each state.

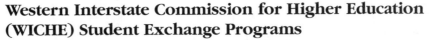

Western Interstate Commission for Higher Education (WICHE) Student Exchange Programs

www.wiche.edu/SEP/

Each year more than 17,000 students in Alaska, Arizona, California, Colorado, Hawaii, Idaho, Montana, Nevada, New Mexico, North Dakota, Oregon, South Dakota, Utah, Washington, and Wyoming participate in this exchange program, which offers significant savings on out-of-state tuition among these Western states. Undergraduates, graduate students, and professional students can find out whether their field of study is supported, find a list of schools, and learn how to apply.

General Information on Postsecondary Education

You'll find even more information on all aspects of postsecondary education at the next few sites.

Back to College

www.back2college.com

Back to College, an extensive Web site for returning students, contains information and links to topics from admissions to financial aid to finding a program. "Ask the Experts" your questions about going back to college, or talk with other returnees in the online forums. You can also sign up for a free monthly e-mail newsletter. Check out the site map for an organized breakdown of the subjects covered.

The Center For All Collegiate Information

www.collegiate.net

The Center For All Collegiate Information is a comprehensive portal that serves as a one-stop directory for all aspects of postsecondary education. Sponsored by Aphco International, this Web site organizes college-related sites into areas from financial aid to graduate programs to distance-learning opportunities.

HEATH Resource Center

www.heath.gwu.edu

George Washington University's HEATH Resource Center serves as a comprehensive clearinghouse on postsecondary education for students with disabilities. Read the quarterly newsletter and other free publications, browse the resource directory to find contacts for specific issues, or get answers to the most frequently asked questions on educational issues for people with disabilities.

U.S. Department of Education

www.ed.gov/index.jsp

Where else would you turn for information on education than the U.S. Department of Education? Its higher-education, career, and lifelong learning sections are most applicable here. Find out about planning and paying for an education, as well as government initiatives, research, and statistics to help you find out more about postsecondary education in general. You can also order popular publications online, or download free brochures such as the yearly Student Guide to Financial Aid.

CHAPTER 2

Distance Learning and Lifelong Learning

Think you know all about distance learning? Now's the time to ditch any outdated ideas you might have about taking correspondence courses by mail. Today, the most important innovations in distance learning are expanding everyone's ability to learn over the Internet, through organizations, companies, or universities.

Online learning is appealing because it is accessible anytime and anywhere students have access to the Web. What better way to fit education into our ever-more-hectic lives? The Web sites in this chapter take you through a number of distance-learning options, either for earning a college degree or as part of your lifelong learning strategy.

Lifelong learning is critical both in the workplace and as a part of your development as an employee and an individual. In the workplace, especially, employers need to maintain a well-trained staff, so employees must sharpen their skills to stay current or get ahead in their fields. For both groups, training must be available, cost-effective, and convenient.

Although companies still use traditional training methods, online learning is becoming more popular. In this chapter, you'll find out about both on- and offline lifelong learning and degree options, in the workplace and at home. Take the time to make the right choices for the way you learn best. Online learning (sometimes also called e-learning) is emphasized, but you also can find out about other options such as teleconferencing and video courses.

Learning About Distance Learning

Before you jump into trying distance-learning courses for yourself, you might want to learn more about the whole concept. The portal sites in this section provide a good starting point for your exploration.

About Distance Learning

http://distancelearn.about.com

About.com's distance-learning section contains information on all aspects of the subject. Start with the FAQs and Introduction to find out more about distance learning in general and then explore categorized links and articles. Links open in frames, but there is an option to turn off the top advertising bar.

Distance Education Clearinghouse

www.uwex.edu/disted/

The University of Wisconsin-Extension provides the Distance Education Clearinghouse, a comprehensive directory of online resources on distance learning. Its clearly annotated links are broken into a number of useful categories, including definitions, other distance-education sites, journals and readings, organizations and associations, virtual universities, and job opportunities for distance-education instructors. Check out the Student Readiness section for resources on assessing your own learning style and becoming a successful distance learner.

Distance Learning On the Net

www.hoyle.com/distance.htm

In addition to extensive links to specific distance-learning institutions and courses, Glenn Hoyle provides links to other distance-learning portals, organizations, teaching resources, conferences, vendors, and so on. Distance Learning On the Net is a winner of the Britannica Internet Guide Award. Hoyle's list of new links can give you an idea of what is currently happening in the field of distance education.

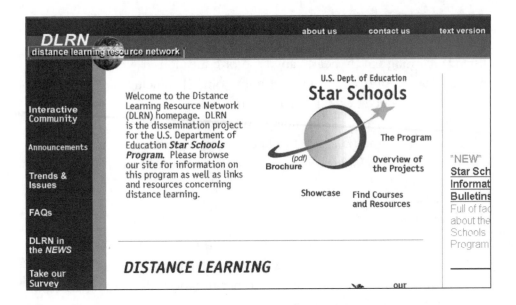

Distance Learning Resource Network (DLRN)

www.dlrn.org

> DLRN is intended to support the federally funded Star Schools distance-education program. It provides a plethora of information on distance learning in general. There are sections geared toward K–12 students (including a list of "virtual schools"), adult learners, and educators, as well as a library of distance-education resources. Check out the Trends and Issues link for hot topics in distance learning.

What Makes a Successful Online Student?

http://illinois.online.uillinois.edu/IONresources/onlineLearning/
StudentProfile.asp

> Before you spend the money to enroll yourself in a distance-learning program, especially an online program, take the time to discover if your learning style fits well with the distance-learning environment, and see whether your computing equipment meets technical requirements. This site provides questions to ask yourself as well as links to interactive quizzes that evaluate your readiness to learn online. You'll also find advice on succeeding as an online learner.

Distance-Learning Directories

Distance learning covers nearly any type of education in which you and an instructor are not present in the same room. This includes classes using audiotapes or videotapes, teleconferencing and videoconferencing, and computer and Internet-based training. Although many of these directories reflect the growing popularity of online learning options, you can find information on other distance-education opportunities as well.

Degree.net

www.degree.net

This companion Web site to *Bears' Guide to Earning Degrees by Distance Learning* and other distance-learning guides includes columns, news stories, links to other distance-education sites, and much more. Be sure to investigate the extensive accreditation information to get the background you need to evaluate distance-learning schools and courses. This site also includes information on 100 recommended distance-learning schools.

Distance.Gradschools.com

http://distance.gradschools.com

If you have already graduated from college, you might be contemplating furthering your education by pursuing a graduate degree. Distance graduate programs make it easier for working adults to earn graduate degrees in a number of areas, and Distance.Gradschools.com allows you to locate programs by course of study. Each listing contains contact information for a particular school, and some link to the school's Web site for further information on the program.

Distance Learning Course Finder

www.dlcoursefinder.com

The Distance Learning Course Finder includes more than 55,000 distance-learning courses and programs from universities, colleges, and companies worldwide. Locate courses in your area of interest by searching by keyword, subject, country, or institution name. Then answer a few questions, such as your preferred method of delivery (Internet, video, and so on) and whether you are looking for a degree-granting program. You'll also find links to distance-education articles, reports, and associations.

Globewide Network Academy (GNA)

www.gnacademy.org

GNA's extensive course catalog lists distance-learning courses and degree programs worldwide. Browse by your area of interest or search by keyword to find links to specific courses and programs. Certificate programs, continuing education, nondegree, and degree programs are all included. The Student Channel includes helpful articles, links, and information for those considering pursuing distance-learning opportunities.

Petersons.com: Distance Learning

www.petersons.com/distancelearning/

Search for your distance program of interest from among the 1,100 included here by name of school, keyword, or degree, or find continuing education online opportunities. You'll find detailed descriptions of most of the colleges, as well as contact info and links to their Web sites. Also explore Petersons' online learning self-assessment and links to distance-learning consortia. See chapter 1 for more on Petersons.com.

USNews.com: Education: E-Learning

www.usnews.com/usnews/edu/elearning/elhome.htm

USNews.com's searchable e-learning directory includes more than 2,000 regionally accredited institutions offering distance course-work for credit. You also can investigate information on "the best" online graduate degree programs in business, engineering, education, public health, and library science, as well as a number of US News articles on distance education. Nice features here include an online discussion forum and profiles of successful online students.

WorldWideLearn

www.worldwidelearn.com

WorldWideLearn bills itself as "the World's largest directory of online courses, accredited online degrees, online training, and online education"—and there's certainly a lot to explore here! Browse online degree programs, courses, and training programs by subject, or look at continuing education opportunities by field of specialty (from accounting to veterinary). You can also sign up for a free monthly e-mail newsletter on online learning or explore a number of free online tutorials.

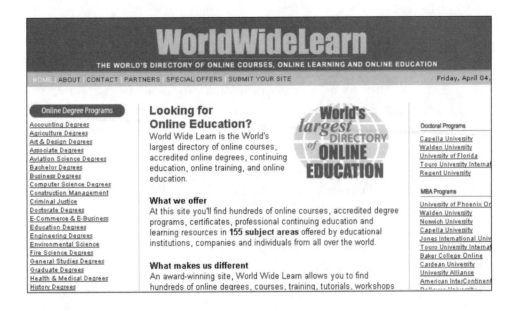

Distance-Learning Career and Degree Institutions

This section offers a closer look at some institutions that offer distance-learning programs. Realize that these are just examples. So many schools now offer at least some distance-learning opportunities that you might want to first locate your ideal school and then see whether you can learn at a distance through them. If you do choose to pursue a degree or take courses at a distance, especially online, realize that you have the added advantage of preparing for employer-based online learning later in your career. This is becoming an essential part of employee training at many companies.

If you are interested in pursuing an undergraduate or graduate degree, make sure that the institution you choose is accredited, and investigate its reputation. Although the Internet has made it easier to find distance opportunities, unfortunately it has also made it easier for unscrupulous organizations to set up "schools" that take advantage of unsuspecting students.

Education Direct

www.educationdirect.com

Education Direct specializes in distance career programs for adult learners. They focus on career diploma programs, from child day care management to court reporter to pharmacy technician. They also offer associate's degrees in selected areas. Choose an area of interest to receive a free information packet by mail, and then enroll in a program to receive self-study materials at home. Proceed through modules and take exams online, by mail, or by phone at your own pace.

Jones International University

www.jonesinternational.edu

Jones International, the first accredited fully online university, offers undergraduate, graduate, and certificate programs to distance learners. View the online demo to see an interactive Flash movie tour of the process. Each new student receives an online orientation to JIU, including instruction on using class Web pages and discussion forums, and peer and academic advisors are available via e-mail. You can also enroll in courses for continuing education purposes without enrolling in a degree program.

National University Online

http://online.nu.edu

The third-largest private university in California, National University offers teaching credentials, certificates, and a number of graduate and undergraduate degree programs geared toward busy working adults. Check out their online demo course to see what an actual course looks like, read about their awards and accreditations to reassure yourself about online learning, and apply online.

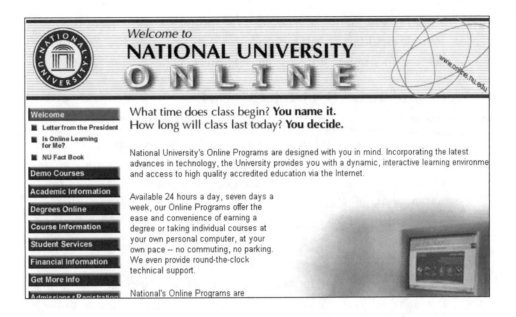

University of Missouri-Columbia High School (MU)

http://cdis.missouri.edu/MUHighschool/HShome.htm

Want an accredited four-year diploma—your high school diploma, that is? MU High School offers more than 150 accredited high school courses for independent learners. Take courses online and apply the credit at your own high school, investigate classes not available in your area, catch up on courses, find courses for gifted students, supplement a homeschooling curriculum, or earn your diploma entirely online. Offered by the University of Missouri's Center for Distance and Independent Study.

University of Phoenix

www.phoenix.edu

The nation's largest private university, the University of Phoenix gears its accredited graduate and undergraduate degree programs toward working adults. You have the option of learning entirely online; taking in-person courses near you at one of their 117 campuses across the U.S., Canada, and Puerto Rico; or using a combination of both to complete your degree. Browse the site to find out about degrees offered and financial aid/scholarship options.

Their current fact book provides useful information about the school, including faculty information, student statistics, and information on student services and campuses.

University of Texas (UT) TeleCampus

www.telecampus.utsystem.edu

UT offers undergraduate, masters, and certificate programs—all online—as well as a searchable database of classes offered by any UT campus through any distance-education method. Texas high school students should be sure to check out the dual-credit program, where they can enroll in online classes and receive both high school and college credit. UT's online fact book provides information similar to that offered by the University of Phoenix (just discussed). Student services offers 24-hour technical support, financial aid information and contacts, free online tutoring, and other useful services.

Walden University

www.waldenu.edu

Walden University offers programs in four academic areas: education, health and human services, management, and psychology. Sign up to request a free virtual tour on CD-ROM, find out about average time requirements to finish each online degree, and browse financial aid options. Most programs have minimal in-person residency requirements, but Walden has a number of satellite locations around the U.S. for your convenience.

Western Governors University

www.wgu.edu/wgu/

Founded by the governors of several western states, Western Governors' program uses a unique competency-based (rather than credit-based) system. Take their assessment tests to put your existing skills and experience to work toward earning a degree, even if you have no previous college experience. The school offers distance-learning courses from colleges and corporations across the U.S., using various methods of delivery.

Distance-Learning Consortia

State or regional distance-learning consortia harness the power of multiple institutions to provide a broad array of classes and options to potential students, generally allowing students enrolled in any one school to take distance-education courses at any other member institution. Again, these are just examples of the variety of consortia out there. Check to see whether your own state or regional board sponsors its own version.

Canadian Virtual University (CVU)

www.cvu-uvc.ca

✓ CVU allows students enrolled in any of 13 participating universities to take more than 2,000 distance courses offered by any of the institutions. As with the interstate student exchange programs described in chapter 1, this system offers significant savings by waiving visiting-student fees for classes taken outside your home university. Search here for degree programs or for individual courses in your area of interest. Degrees are provided through your accredited "home university" rather than through CVU itself.

Electronic Campus (Southern Regional Education Board)

www.electroniccampus.org

✓ The Southern Regional Education Board (SREB) sponsors this collection of electronic courses and programs from hundreds of accredited colleges and universities in the 16 SREB states. (For more on SREB, see chapter 1.) A number of courses are available at an "electronic tuition rate," which offers significant savings over out-of-state tuition. Search for individual courses or for entire programs of study, or do a side-by-side comparison to see how similar programs compare at different institutions.

Kentucky Virtual University (KVU)

www.kcvu.org

✓ This virtual campus offers both online degree programs and professional education courses provided by a number of colleges, universities, and institutions statewide. Degrees are awarded by the college or university rather than by KVU itself. You'll also find links to the Kentucky Virtual High School, Virtual Library, and Virtual Adult Education initiative. You can also sign up to be notified by e-mail about new programs, classes, and services.

National Universities Degree Consortium (NUDC)

www.nudc.org

Distance-learning graduate and undergraduate degrees from NUDC's accredited member institutions are available to any U.S. student, and classes are given through a variety of delivery methods (including the Internet, audio and video, printed self-study materials, CD-ROM, and teleconferences). Find out which participating institutions offer which degrees, search for courses, and apply for financial aid online.

SUNY Learning Network

http://SLN.suny.edu

The State University of New York's online program offers more than 1,500 courses through 53 participating universities to allow students to complete their degree (or just a few courses) on their

own time, at their own convenience. Start with the Prospective Students link for all the information you need to get started, including answers to frequently asked questions; financial aid, registration, and tuition information; degree programs; and a distance-learning savings calculator.

Looking for Learning in All the Right Places: Continuing Education

Beyond working toward a degree, lifelong learners also have a number of distance-education opportunities. Remember to check the distance-learning directories discussed earlier for additional noncredit opportunities. Noncredit courses are often referred to as continuing or professional education classes. Although some of the sites in this section concentrate on particular specialties or professions, others include courses in a variety of areas. Courses are available for those just wanting to shore up their skills or learn new things, as well as for those needing to meet continuing-education requirements in their company or profession. On- and offline lifelong learning opportunities include seminars, online courses, videos, programs, and workshops in a number of areas.

Barnes & Noble University

www.barnesandnobleuniversity.com

Online classes from a bookstore? Why not? Most courses here are free, and they offer interaction with an instructor and fellow students through online forums. Barnes & Noble makes its money selling you required textbooks, but you are under no obligation to buy from them. Subject areas include liberal arts, information technology, graphic and Web design, writing and languages, life improvement, and business and office productivity.

OnlineLearning.net

www.OnlineLearning.net

Busy teachers looking to meet professional development continuing education requirements or lifelong learning objectives should investigate this site's online options. Choose from 20 different subject areas, from Praxis study to character education to teaching English as a foreign language. You can also sign up with this site to create a personal start page and receive information on new courses and upcoming events.

Prometheon

www.seminarfinder.com

Prometheon has easy-to-find listings—not only of publicly available in-person seminars, but also of continuing-education programs and Web-based training. You can browse the listings by topic or city or search for specific offerings. You can also browse the forums or read free articles on common seminar topics such as coaching, small business, and personal improvement.

Seminar Information Service

www.seminarinformation.com

If distance learning isn't your thing, the Seminar Information Service provides an easy way to search for more than 360,000 live, in-person seminars, classes, workshops, conferences, and corporate training events annually. Search by keyword, location, date, or

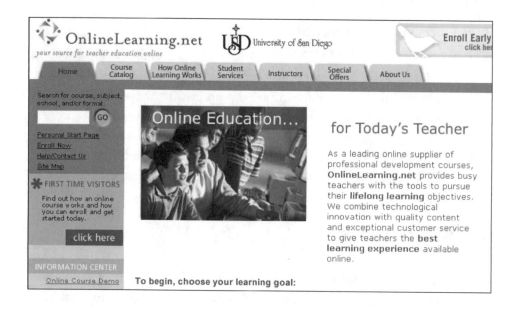

topic, browse featured events, or browse by subject area to see information on events and speakers. Many seminars provide the option to enroll online. You can also subscribe to a monthly e-mail newsletter to find out about new seminars and read free articles.

TeleClass.com

www.teleclass.com

For a unique distance-learning experience, try TeleClass.com. Classes take place by live conference call, allowing you to interact with an instructor and other students from all over. All you need is a phone line and a willingness to pay long-distance charges! Many classes are free, and others are offered for a minimal fee. Course areas include coaching and consulting, Internet, professional development, certifications, money, small business, marriage/family, training/teaching, writing, corporate, personal development, communication, and marketing.

Military-Sponsored Educational Opportunities

The U.S. military recognizes the importance of education for all service members and sponsors both degree and continuing-education opportunities. A number of these are available online or through other distance-learning methods so that active personnel can learn while serving their country, wherever they may be stationed. For information on joining or working for the military, see chapter 7.

Advanced Learning Technology Resource Center (ALTRC)

www.altrc.org

Cosponsored by the Department of Defense, the National Guard, and the Department of Labor, ALTRC is a one-stop shop that connects government employees and departments with flexible lifelong learning opportunities. Pick the Learners link for information on everything from occupations to training opportunities to financial aid resources. You can also read current distance-learning news and find out about government and military initiatives.

Air Force Institute for Advanced Distributed Learning

www.maxwell.af.mil/au/afiadl/

⌐ The U.S. Air Force manages its own distance-learning program for current personnel. Many courses are taught via satellite broadcasts or computer-assisted instruction. The site lists continuing education and for-credit offerings from a number of related organizations and Air Force divisions. Check out the Site Index for an overview of the comprehensive information contained here.

DANTES Distance Learning Programs

www.dantes.doded.mil

⌐ Through agreements with a number of schools with existing distance-learning programs, DANTES provides distance-learning opportunities to active service members who are in the process of earning their degrees—wherever they are stationed. Nondegree courses are also available for military personnel looking to improve their technical or other skills. Up to 75% of tuition costs can be reimbursed by DANTES or the appropriate service branch upon successful completion of each course.

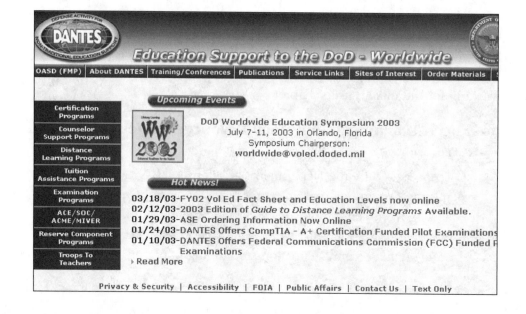

Department of Defense Voluntary Education Program

`http://voled.doded.mil`

✓ The Voluntary Education program provides information on high school, vocational/technical, undergraduate, and graduate educational opportunities for U.S. military personnel. On this site, you find descriptions of available programs for each service branch and links to scholarship and tuition assistance information, fact sheets, certifications, examination info, and much, much more. Also look here for links to information on DANTES (just described).

Distributed Training Technology Project

`www.dttp.ngb.army.mil`

✓ The U.S. National Guard sponsors this cooperative program, which provides computer-based and satellite training opportunities for its personnel via more than 300 multimedia classrooms across the country. Read through news articles to find out more about the program, or find out how to get started in the Student section. Success stories posted on the site give you an idea of the topics that are taught.

eArmyU.com

`www.earmyu.com`

✓ eArmyU offers soldiers anytime, anywhere learning and more than 116 online degree programs through partnerships with more than 21 U.S. universities. First use the eligibility checklist to see whether you qualify for the program, and then browse through the certificates and degrees that are offered, or search the catalog for specific courses in your area of interest. Subjects are broken into several "program communities." Mentors are available to advise students in their area of study. Army personnel can earn credits, certificates, and degrees at a low cost or no cost while remaining on active duty. Each program enrollee receives a technology package for use in his or her studies, including a laptop preloaded with the appropriate software.

Federal Learning eXchange (FLX)

www.flx.gov

FLX bills itself as "a comprehensive searchable database for training and education resources available to federal employees"—and
it lives up to its description. Classes from hundreds of providers
can be searched by keyword or subject. Government employees
(including military personnel) can search by their preferred distance delivery method (such as CD, Web-based, satellite, or correspondence courses).

GI Bill

www.gibill.va.gov

Find out about the educational benefits offered by the GI Bill—
important announcements are posted right on the front page of
the site. You can also use the FAQ to find quick answers to the
most frequently asked questions about the bill, and ask your own
question via an online form if it is not answered there. You can
also print copies of applications and other useful forms and find
current news on rate changes and other program changes.

Navy E-Learning

www.navylearning.com

Navy E-Learning provides Navy and Marine Corps personnel,
retirees, and qualified dependents with online training and professional development opportunities. Use the Catalog link to find out
what courses are currently available, and then investigate the training and professional development links for additional options.

Servicemembers Opportunity Colleges (SOC)

www.soc.aascu.org

This consortium of more than 1,550 colleges and universities
allows U.S. military service members (and their families) to complete associate's and bachelor's degrees, no matter where they are
stationed or how often they move from place to place. Courses
are offered at Army, Navy, and Marine Corps installations or via
distance learning. Member colleges have agreed to accept each

other's transfer credits. Start by reading "Why Participate in an SOC Program?" for basic information on SOC advantages and requirements. Then check out the links for each service branch for descriptions of specific programs, or download the current SOC Guide (in Adobe Acrobat format) for information on each participating institution and applicable policies.

Career Exploration Information

You'll want to learn as much as you can about potential careers to make sure you choose the one that's right for you. Although there are a number of resources for researching any given career, the Web provides a quick and current way to find the salary ranges, required skills and education, and working conditions for nearly any occupation. While researching potential careers, you can also use online self-assessments and tutorials to help determine the careers that best fit your personality and interests.

The general Web sites in this chapter help you start the career exploration process and give you leads to find more information. You'll also want to explore specific sites relating to your chosen occupation, though. Use the search engines and directories outlined in the Introduction to find more.

Many job and resume banks, such as CareerBuilder and Monster, also feature articles and helpful information on career selection and exploration. These sites are grouped elsewhere in this book (see chapter 4). Clearinghouses of career-related links (see chapter 5) are another great resource for identifying general and specific career information on the Web.

Career Planning

Career planning basically means starting the decision-making process by assessing your own knowledge, interests, skills, and personality, exploring potential careers, and figuring out the steps you need to take to get where you want to go. These sites provide a place to start.

Steps for Career Planning

A great place to check for career planning and development information is your local college career center. This section contains examples of the types of materials that are available from career centers.

Career Development eManual

www.cdm.uwaterloo.ca

> Don't know how to begin choosing your career? Start here, let the staff at the University of Waterloo Career Services Office walk you step-by-step through a time-tested planning process, and end up proactively in charge of your own career. Their six steps are Self-Assessment, Research, Decision-Making (including Education), Networks and Contacts, Work, and Life/Work Planning. The getting started quiz shows you which steps you might need to concentrate your efforts on.

Career Exploration Links

www.uhs.berkeley.edu/students/CareerLibrary/links/careerme.htm

> Although Berkeley's Career Exploration Links, sponsored by University Health Services, is aimed at college students, there is useful information here for anyone embarking on the career-planning process. Start with an interest assessment, picking the personality type that seems to match yours most closely, and find out about good majors and careers for your type. Or read brief profiles of actual students whose types match yours. Then read about majors, graduate programs, and career information through the extensive links.

Career Planning Process

`www.bgsu.edu/offices/sa/career/students/planning_process.html`

Bowling Green State University's Career Planning Process outlines a career exploration model designed to help people gain competencies, make decisions, set goals, and take action. The model walks you through several steps: Self-Assessment, Academic/Career Options, Relevant/Practical Experience, Job Search/Graduate School Preparation, and Career Change. Each includes exercises and concrete strategies for further exploration.

JobWeb—Career Development

`www.jobweb.com/Career_Development/`

JobWeb, sponsored by the National Association of Colleges and Employers, has a useful section devoted to the career development process. It divides the process into four steps: Discovery, Exploration, Experience & Experiment, and Choice. Each step includes a number of resources for further investigation. For example, the Discovery section links you to a Career Profile Search, where you can select your major and find out which careers you might be prepared for. Take some time to work through the resources here and explore your many options.

UW Oshkosh Career Services: What Can I Do With a Major In...

www.uwosh.edu/career/whatcanidowithamajorin.html

> What Can I Do With a Major In...provides a list of majors available at the University of Wisconsin, Oshkosh. Pick any major to see a brief description, related links, a list of careers that match that major (with links to information on each from the *Occupational Outlook Handbook*), links to Web sites that list job openings for those types of careers, types of employers that hire graduates with that major, and strategies for success in the field. You'll also find general self-assessment and career-planning tools to help you get started.

Self-Assessment

You might have noticed that the first step in the sites just discussed generally is self-assessment: getting a realistic picture of your skills, interests, personality, values, motivation, knowledge, and abilities. This only makes sense—you need to figure out who you are and what you want before you can make an informed choice about your future (or next) career. But self-exploration can be a daunting task, so the Web sites in this section provide a variety of self-assessment tools to help you start this process. You might want to check out a couple different sites, because each has its own method and own theories of personality.

The Big Five Personality Test

www.outofservice.com/bigfive/

> U.C. Berkeley psychologist Frank J. Sulloway provides this test to measure "the five fundamental dimensions of personality." Its unique feature is that you are encouraged to answer each question both from your own perspective and as another person you know well. Your and the other person's percentile results (as compared to others who have taken this online test) are explained in five areas: Openness to Experience/Intellect, Conscientiousness,

Extraversion, Agreeableness, and Neuroticism. You'll also find links to other personality sites on the Web that let you find out more about the Big Five approach and your results.

The Career Key

www.careerkey.org/english/

This free online self-assessment from North Carolina State University professor emeritus Lawrence K. Jones is intended to help visitors choose a career or college major, change careers, or plan a career. Take the quiz to measure your skills, abilities, interests, and personality; use it to identify jobs that match your profile; find out more about those jobs; and learn how to take concrete steps toward achieving the career goal(s) you identify. The test is based on Holland's Theory of Career Choice.

Enneagram Institute

www.enneagraminstitute.com

Learn about the Enneagram theory of nine personality types at this Web site, and then take a free short sample test that might identify yours. You can then read your personality profile to learn about the healthy and unhealthy features of your type, your motivations, and examples of famous individuals who share the same type. You'll also find recommendations for "personal growth" targeted specifically at your type. You have the option to purchase a fuller test for more accurate results.

International Assessment Network: MAPP

www.assessment.com

MAPP stands for Motivational Analysis of Personal Potential. Here you explore your career interests based on understanding what motivates you. Register for free to take a sample assessment intended to identify your real motivations, interests, and talents. Your results and supporting material, including five job descriptions, are e-mailed to you. Intrigued by the sample results? You can purchase a longer report and additional information.

Keirsey Temperament and Character Web Site

www.keirsey.com

Although much of this site is devoted to advertising Keirsey's books and related material, you can also register for free to take the Keirsey Temperament Sorter II. You're provided with a free brief description of your temperament type, along with the opportunity to purchase further results. The test is available in multiple languages. After taking the test, go back to the main page to find examples of famous people who share your personality type, read excerpts from Keirsey's work, and find out about the typical vocational interests of different temperaments.

Informational Interviewing

One of the best ways to learn more about the real-world aspects of a given career is by talking to people currently working in the field. This section shows you how.

Information Interviews (Florida State University)

www.career.fsu.edu/ccis/guides/infoint.html

This site is a nice summary overview of the informational interviewing process, including why to do one, whom you should contact, where you can find these people, and how you should prepare for your informational interview. You'll also find ideas on questions you can ask and information on how you should go about setting up the interview.

Quintessential Careers: Informational Interviewing Tutorial

www.quintcareers.com/informational_interviewing.html

As opposed to job interviewing, informational interviewing is intended to help you find out about working in a field and begin building a network of others in the same occupation. This tutorial walks you through the informational interview process, from

identifying people to interview to doing your homework before-
hand to evaluating the information you receive. You'll also find a
ton of sample questions to spark your thoughts on what you might
ask your contact.

U.S. Department of Labor Career Information

The U.S. Department of Labor (DOL) is the lead federal agency for
employment-related programs and statistics. It shares its research and
information with all job seekers through several comprehensive Web sites.

America's Career InfoNet

www.acinet.org/acinet/

America's Career InfoNet (ACINet), a federal-state partnership, is
designed to help citizens make more informed career decisions.
Use the information here to learn about wages and employment
trends in particular occupations in your state; find out what education, skills, and abilities are needed; search for employer contact
information; and browse links to thousands of other online career
resources. Here's just a sampling of what you'll find: Pick the What
It Takes link to learn what skills and abilities are required in different fields, and watch free online videos on the occupation; pick
the State Information link for a report on the average income,
unemployment rate, and fastest-growing occupations in your state;
pick Wages and Trends to see information on average salaries and
the outlook for your selected occupation in your selected state.

Career Guide to Industries

www.bls.gov/oco/cg/

The DOL's Bureau of Labor Statistics' *Career Guide to Industries* allows you to locate career information by industry. Just select a broad category from the links on the right, or choose the A–Z Index to search for a particular industry by name. Information on each includes the nature of the industry, working conditions, employment, occupations in the industry, training and advancement, earnings and benefits, employment outlook, and lists of organizations that can provide additional information. You might want to start with the "How Industries Differ" page for an overview of how understanding current industry conditions can help you find the job outlook and employment conditions for each. This is a companion guide to the *Occupational Outlook Handbook* (discussed next).

Occupational Outlook Handbook

www.bls.gov/oco/

Every two years, the Bureau of Labor Statistics produces the *Occupational Outlook Handbook*—one of the best-known and most comprehensive books on occupations. The online version contains the same information as the printed copy, sans illustrations. The best way to find details on a particular occupation is to search by job title. Each description provides information on the nature of the work you would be performing, working conditions, links to related occupations, employment statistics, training and education needed, advancement potential, job outlook, earnings, and sources of additional information. You can read online or download a printer-friendly (.PDF) version of each report. Don't have a specific title in mind? Browse by broad category (construction, professional, armed forces, and so on) to access a list of job titles, and then read about those that interest you.

O*NET

http://online.onetcenter.org

O*NET, the Occupational Information Network, contains comprehensive information on job requirements and competencies. Search for occupations by title, keyword, or field, or use the skills checklists to find occupations that use your existing skills. After you look up an occupation, read a brief description, request further details, or search for related jobs to get ideas on other directions to take your career. Because O*NET is intended to provide standardized information to job seekers and employers, each description takes the same format and includes the same types of information.

Career Information Potpourri

You can find a mix of career exploration information from a variety of sources: career columnists and authors, online newspapers and magazines, publishers, agencies, and more.

American Society of Association Executives (ASAE) Gateway to Association Web Sites

`http://info.asaenet.org/gateway/OnlineAssocsList.html`

> Professional associations generally contain quite a bit of information on a given occupation, from the perspective of actual members of that profession. ASAE's directory can be searched by association name keyword, category, and city. Jump directly to each association's Web site for further information, which often includes educational suggestions, member services, conference information, an outline of the specialty, and more.

Ask the Headhunter

www.asktheheadhunter.com

> This site boldly begins by stating, "America's Employment System is broken. Everything you know about job hunting and hiring is wrong. Throw away your resume or job description and Ask the Headhunter." You'll find nontraditional advice on setting yourself apart from the competition and beating the system. You can read free articles, sign up for an e-mail newsletter, or ask the headhunter your own questions on an online message board (a paid subscription is required).

Barbara Sher

www.barbarasher.com

> Best-selling career author Barbara Sher's Web site includes success stories and articles, offers for small-group teleclasses, and a free e-mail newsletter. You'll also find ideas on starting your own "Success Team" with friends or finding a certified team leader near you. (Members of Success Teams support each other in achieving their individual dreams.) The outstanding feature is Sher's active online forums, where you can find topics ranging from success stories to job hunting to "needs and links." Your questions can be answered either by fellow members or by Sher herself.

CareerJournal.com

www.careerjournal.com

> With a name like the *Wall Street Journal* behind it, you know that CareerJournal.com is a site loaded with all sorts of career information and articles. Find daily feature career articles, search the database of free and low-cost events, join discussion boards, and read special reports. You can also sign up to personalize the site so that it defaults to showing articles and job postings matching your interests, add your resume to the database, or sign up for customized e-mail job listings. Click the site map link to access all articles and resources by subject area.

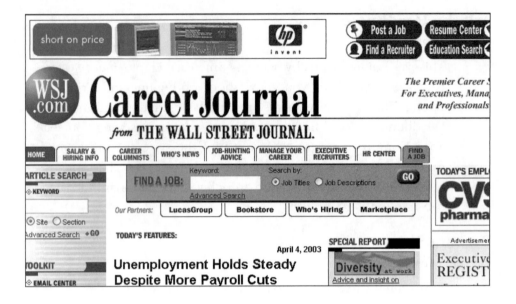

Careers in Business

www.careers-in-business.com

> A straightforward name for a straightforward site: Careers in
> Business focuses on all aspects of exploring common business
> careers. Choose from occupational areas from accounting to non-
> profit to find an overview of the profession, skills needed, job
> options, salaries, links to other sites, trends, top firms, and recom-
> mended books on the subject. Scroll down the main page for a list
> of links to other recommended career sites.

Careers On-Line (University of Montana Disability Services)

http://ds.umn.edu

> As a federally funded project based at the University of Minnesota,
> Careers On-Line's information for people with disabilities is most
> applicable to Minnesotans, but the site also includes more-general
> resources. The most important link here is to job accommodation
> information, which includes a link to the DOL's Job Accommoda-
> tion Network, a handbook listing case studies of UM graduates
> who were successfully accommodated on the job, and telecommut-
> ing resources.

Federal Consumer Information Center: Employment

www.pueblo.gsa.gov/textver/t_employ.htm

The Federal Consumer Information Center offers some straightforward background information on several career exploration topics. On this site, you can order low-cost brochures on various employment issues or read them online and print them for free. Topics include apprenticeships, interviewing, the job outlook for various occupations, and work-at-home scams. You can also find some useful related links.

Find Your Spot

www.findyourspot.com

Take a quiz on your preferences and attitudes to find the perfect "spot" in which to live, and then get a list of top spots and information on each—including job listings from FlipDog. (Registration is required to see the list of spots.) For each of your matching spots, find the cost of living, population, weather, housing costs, educational information, and updates on the local economy, and then opt to find jobs in those spots. Don't like your list? Go back and change your quiz answers, or remove individual spots, and the next best matches are added. Also connect with the site's partner relocation agents to help find homes in your ideal cities.

JIST Publishing

www.jist.com

JIST Publishing is a good resource for career, job search, business, and self-help career assessments, workbooks, books, reference books, videos, and software. The site includes information on all JIST materials and secure online ordering, plus links to online career assessments, thorough occupational data, career news, tips, and many other career Web sites. You can sign up for free catalogs and a free quarterly newsletter.

JobProfiles.org

`www.jobprofiles.org`

For firsthand accounts from successful individuals in a variety of careers, visit JobProfiles.org. Each profile highlights the rewards, stresses, skills, and challenges of the career, and individuals provide advice on entering the field. Browse by category or search for profiles by keyword. You'll also find an introductory article on successfully researching and managing your career. Use the opinions in these profiles to supplement more-general information, along the lines of an informational interview.

JobStar

`http://jobstar.org`

A public-library-produced guide to job searching and career exploration, JobStar focuses on localized information for California job seekers, but it contains plenty of resources useful to career planners everywhere. This Web site contains links to hundreds of general and profession-specific salary surveys and salary negotiation strategies, career guides for a number of specific careers, free online career tests, information on the "hidden" job market and on researching companies, "Ask Electra," an expert advice section, and more.

Licensed Occupations Tool

`www.acinet.org/acinet/lois_start.asp`

ACINet's Licensed Occupations Tool lets you look through occupational licensing requirements by state, occupation, or agency. This helps you get an idea of how licensing requirements differ by state and what you might have to do when relocating or beginning a career in a particular place. For further information, find contact information for the state licensing agencies for particular occupations.

Planning a Career

`www.mapping-your-future.org/planning/`

> Although it's aimed at potential college students, Planning a Career can be useful to anyone wanting information on choosing and beginning a career. Their ten straightforward steps to planning your career are Develop a career plan, Assess your skills and interests, Research occupations, Compare your skills and interests with these occupations, Choose your career goal, Select a school, Find out about financial aid, Get job hunting tips, Prepare your resume and practice interviewing techniques, and Get more information. Each step links to more information and tips.

WetFeet.com

`www.wetfeet.com`

> WetFeet.com's goal is "helping you make smarter career decisions"—and there's a ton of info here to help you do just that! You'll find information on companies, careers, and industries. You'll benefit from expert advice, newsletters, salary tools, and online discussions. Each category links to related categories and a matching discussion board for further exploration. Special sections are devoted to undergrads, MBAs, and career changers. Free registration is required to access a number of the site's features.

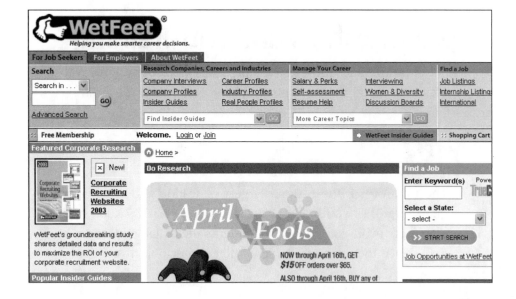

Career-Related Organizations for High School Students

In-school programs like those described at the following site can be a great way to explore your options before graduation. Find out about different programs and see whether they are available in your school. Also use the search engines discussed in the Introduction to find student organizations in your particular area of interest.

Career & Technical Student Organizations

www.acteonline.org/resource_center/student-org.cfm

> This page from the Association for Career and Technical Education (ACTE) Web site is a handy list of links to career and technical student organizations. These include such groups as Business Professionals of America, Technology Students Association, and Distributive Education Clubs of America. Membership in career and technical student organizations can give students learning opportunities and experiences beyond the classroom, including competitions, conferences, and state and national recognition. Several organizations provide information on starting a chapter in your own school.

Apprenticeships and Job Training

Apprenticeship programs and the Job Corps mix classroom work with on-the-job training and provide entryways into high-skill, rewarding professions.

Job Corps

http://jobcorps.doleta.gov

> The Job Corps is the nation's largest education and training program for at-risk youth ages 16–24. It serves nearly 70,000 students a year. Its main goal is to give students the skills, education, and experience they need to achieve their career objectives. Find out

about the program, eligibility requirements, and interview process online, and then call the 800 number to get your questions answered and be referred to a local admissions counselor, or e-mail for a free brochure. The locations link gives contact and Web site information for the office(s) in your state. If you've already gone through the program, you can join the National Job Corps Alumni Association.

Office of Apprenticeship Training, Employer and Labor Services

www.doleta.gov/atels_bat/

This DOL-sponsored site serves both individuals looking for apprenticeships and employers seeking to set up apprenticeship programs. This is your source of general information about what an apprenticeship entails and its benefits, as well as links to places to find a program. Apprenticeships teach a trade through a combination of on-the-job training and related instruction. They can be one of the best ways to learn the ins and outs of a particular occupation.

Salary Information

Use the sites in this section to learn the average pay rates in your chosen field, get tips on salary negotiation, and find cost-of-living information for different parts of the country. Knowing what different fields pay can help you make an informed career decision.

Abbott, Langer & Associates

www.abbott-langer.com

You can find free summary data, including median salaries, from the various salary surveys that Abott, Langer & Associates conducts. This site contains current statistics for more than 470 benchmark jobs and from more than 7,000 participating organizations. Select from major fields, such as accounting, information technology, and engineering, and then choose from the surveys available for each field. Your organization can also sign up to participate in upcoming salary surveys to receive discounts on full reports.

JobStar Salary Information

http://jobstar.org/tools/salary/

Although it's tempting to jump directly to JobStar's more than 300 links to general and profession-specific salary surveys, also take some time to explore salary-negotiation strategies and test your own salary IQ. Information on print resources you might want to check out is also included. The site links to California libraries, but you can look up these books in your own local public library.

Quintessential Careers: Salary-Negotiation Tools

www.quintcareers.com/salary_negotiation.html

You have that job offer in hand—now how can you be sure that you negotiate the salary you deserve? Get inside information and tips at Quintessential Careers' salary-negotiation tutorial on getting the best possible salary, turning unacceptable offers into acceptable ones, handling salary discussions during an interview, and more. You'll also find useful articles on negotiation techniques. You can take an online quiz to see how your negotiating techniques stack up and follow links to other salary-negotiation guides.

The Salary Calculator

www.homefair.com/calc/salcalc.html

Thinking about relocating for a job? Compare the cost of living among hundreds of U.S. and international cities with this handy salary calculator. Just enter your salary and current location, and then select another city to find out what you'll need to make there to sustain the same standard of living. While here, check out other relocation tools as well.

SalaryExpert

`www.salaryexpert.com`

Find free regional salary reports by selecting your job title and then your zip code or city. Reports list the position's average salary, benefits, and bonuses; show how salaries in a given area compare to the national average; provide a brief description of the occupation; give the average cost of living in the area; and list links to salary info for related jobs. Also available here are selected feature articles and international salary reports.

Wageweb

`www.wageweb.com`

Although Wageweb is geared toward employers needing to know competitive wages in order to retain employees, individuals can also find useful salary information here. This site provides national salary information for more than 170 benchmark positions, broken down by category and then by job title.

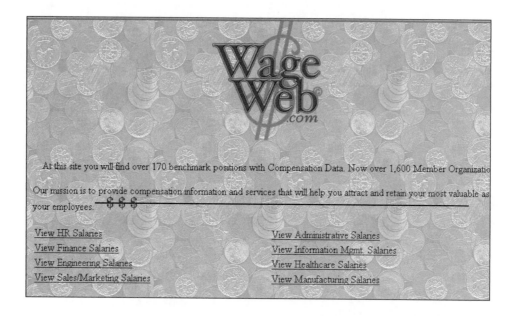

CHAPTER 4

Finding and Applying for Job Openings

If you've read this far straight through the book, you've shown great determination to establish your career path! Your reward comes now, as you'll learn about a number of great places to look for job openings online. Now that you've researched your educational options and decided on a potential career path, the sites in this chapter include national, regional, and industry-specific job banks and government employment sources. After you've used these job banks to find openings, information on resumes and interviewing will help you land that perfect position.

There is no shortage of job information on the Internet. Employers know that recruiting online is one of the easiest ways to quickly reach large numbers of potential applicants, and job seekers can narrow down the most relevant listings without having to page through each Sunday's paper.

Internet job bank Monster alone is the 16th most-visited site on the entire Web. On a typical day, more than four million Americans look for job information online. More employers are using the Web to post open positions and screen candidates as well. Although "techie" jobs predominated just a couple of years ago, now the jobs listed online are becoming more diverse, reflecting companies' growing Internet savvy and the diversity of the Internet audience.

The numbers can be overwhelming. If you're job hunting, though, the only important number is one—the one best job for you. Use the resources in this chapter to start narrowing down your search and learn to go beyond Monster with some of the other great online job banks at your disposal.

Many job banks also include resume banks for employers to peruse. For information on creating and posting your electronic resume to job banks and employer Web sites, see the Introduction to this book, as well as the resume sites listed in this chapter. Some sites will e-mail your resume to a potential employer only with your permission. In many, you can block certain companies (such as your current employer) from accessing your information.

More and more job banks now require job seekers to register with at least an e-mail address and name before using their services, usually for no fee. Some request more extensive information, using it to compile a demographic snapshot of their customers and elicit more business from employers and advertisers. Others might share your contact information with vendors. Look for a privacy policy regarding the use of your personal information. If privacy is an issue for you, use a job bank whose policies you are comfortable with. The choice is yours—and you have a lot to choose from!

Government Sources of Job Information

Ever wonder what the government does with your tax dollars? Among other things, both state and federal governments sponsor employment-related Internet sites that can link you to a number of relevant job listings. (For information on jobs with the government itself, see chapter 7's section on civilian military careers and the listings in the section "Other Specialized Job Banks" later in this chapter.)

U.S. Department of Labor

You might remember from chapters 2 and 3 that the Department of Labor provides extensive career-planning resources online. This section tells you about the last component in the DOL's CareerOneStop toolkit, America's Job Bank.

America's Job Bank (AJB)

www.ajb.dni.us

> The flagship component in the DOL's CareerOneStop toolkit, America's Job Bank (AJB) offers a database of more than one million job listings, resume-creation and -posting services, and an automated job scout for job seekers—although you have to register for full functionality. Search by job category, title, keyword, degree or certificate required, military-only, or posting number. You can also limit searches to within 50 miles of your zip code. The "State Gateway" feature leads you to a list of job resources in your own state, for easy access to state job banks, apprenticeship programs, welfare-to-work programs, training providers, and more. You'll also find comprehensive links to other job banks and employment sites, resources for unemployed workers, and employment service offices near you. Because AJB, unlike most commercial services, is free to employers as well as job seekers, it can contain a broader selection of listings than other resources.

State Government Sources

Each state has an agency that oversees its employment service and job-training programs. The names vary from state to state, such as Department of Labor and Industry, Department of Workforce Preparation, or Commission on Employment Security. Many of the jobs posted with each state's employment service are also posted in America's Job Bank, but not all of them. In-state teaching positions and jobs in state government, for example, are two possible exceptions.

In addition to job postings, these agencies are a good starting point to find out more about federal job training programs, unemployment insurance, veterans' programs, and other services for which you might qualify. Note that states tend to move their Web pages around. If the sites in the following table appear to have changed, try going to www.state.*XX*.us, where *XX* is the two-letter postal abbreviation for your state. Then use the links on your state's Web site to locate your employment service program.

State	Web Address
Alabama	http://es.dir.alabama.gov
Alaska	www.labor.state.ak.us
Arizona	www.de.state.az.us/tp/portalq.asp
Arkansas	www.state.ar.us/esd/
California	http://wwwedd.cahwnet.gov
Colorado	www.coworkforce.com/Emp/
Connecticut	www.ctdol.state.ct.us
Delaware	www.delawareworks.com
District of Columbia	http://does.ci.washington.dc.us
Florida	www2.myflorida.com/les/
Georgia	www.dol.state.ga.us/job_ops.htm
Hawaii	http://dlir.state.hi.us
Idaho	www.labor.state.id.us
Illinois	www.ides.state.il.us
Indiana	www.in.gov/dwd/
Iowa	www.iowaworkforce.org
Kansas	www.accesskansas.org/working/
Kentucky	www.kycwd.org
Louisiana	www.ldol.state.la.us/laworks.asp
Maine	www.mainecareercenter.com
Maryland	www.dllr.state.md.us/employment/jobserv.html
Massachusetts	www.detma.org
Michigan	www.Michigan.gov/mdcd/
Minnesota	www.mnwfc.org
Mississippi	www.mesc.state.ms.us

State	Web Address
Missouri	www.works.state.mo.us
Montana	http://dli.state.mt.us
Nebraska	www.dol.state.ne.us
Nevada	www.detr.state.nv.us
New Hampshire	www.nhes.state.nh.us
New Jersey	www.wnjpin.state.nj.us
New Mexico	www.dol.state.nm.us
New York	www.labor.state.ny.us
North Carolina	www.ncesc.com
North Dakota	http://discovernd.com/employment
Ohio	www.state.oh.us/odjfs/
Oklahoma	www.oesc.state.ok.us
Oregon	www.emp.state.or.us
Pennsylvania	www.pacareerlink.state.pa.us
Rhode Island	www.det.state.ri.us
South Carolina	www.sces.org
South Dakota	www.state.sd.us/dol/dol.asp
Tennessee	www.state.tn.us/labor-wfd/
Texas	www.twc.state.tx.us
Utah	http://jobs.utah.gov
Vermont	www.det.state.vt.us
Virginia	www.vec.state.va.us
Washington	www.wa.gov/esd/
West Virginia	www.state.wv.us/bep/
Wisconsin	www.dwd.state.wi.us
Wyoming	http://wydoe.state.wy.us

General Job Banks

General Internet job banks can contain thousands of listings. They're a great place to get started and find out what types of positions are out there.

4Work.com

`www.4work.com`

Conduct a job search at 4Work.com by location and keyword (skill, industry, or job title), or use the Job Alert! agent to receive daily e-mail updates on new jobs that match your criteria. You can even set up multiple agent profiles if you are interested in more than one type of job. Be sure to take a look at the search tips for hints on conducting a more-effective search, and take advantage of the Find Related Opportunities links when you have found a position listing that matches your requirements. 4Work contains career articles and a directory of career resources for further exploration. It also sponsors 4LaborsofLove.org, a database of volunteer opportunities (see chapter 9).

BestJobsUSA.com

`www.bestjobsusa.com`

A nice feature here is the state site selection option, which includes a separate jobs page focused on each U.S. state. On each of these pages, you can conduct a job search in only that state and find local articles and information. You can also use the general search form to search all job listings or sign up to have matching job opportunities e-mailed to you on a regular basis. Registered job seekers have the option of posting their resume online. BestJobsUSA.com has a masking option to hide your personal identification and contact information, if desired. Through its *Employment Review* magazine connection, BestJobsUSA.com sponsors extensive career-related content such as articles, features on "employers of choice," salary surveys, a relocation guide, and virtual job fairs, as well as a free e-mail newsletter containing tips on mastering today's workplace.

CareerBuilder.com

`www.careerbuilder.com`

CareerBuilder.com, the same people who bring you CareerBuilder-branded Help Wanted sections in Sunday papers across the country, here provides a search engine to more than 400,000 jobs. Search by keyword, city, state, field of interest, company, industry, and/or job type; set up a Personal Search Agent to have matching jobs e-mailed directly to your inbox; and post your resume online (at your choice of three different privacy levels). Need more suggestions? Check out the Career Advice section for expert advice and articles on various job-hunting topics. The New Users section can help you get started and show you what is available on this site. Searching for a job abroad? Check out the Canadian and international jobs sections.

Careerbuzz

`www.careerbuzz.com`

Careerbuzz's motto, "Work Hard, Play Harder," is reflected throughout its site. You find traditional features such as a jobs database, personal search agent, resume and interview tips, and employer information. But you'll also find a Chillin' section that provides trivia contests, horoscopes, and other fun breaks from the job hunt, as well as a Schmooze section that lets you talk to others on online message boards. On the right, you'll find links to current employment-related news stories.

CareerShop.com

`www.careershop.com`

CareerShop tries to harness the power of the Internet to automate the job search and career-management process as much as possible for both job seekers and employers. Search for a job by category, keyword, or location; access the Ask the Career Dr. career

advice; use the Personal Job Shopper to have matching jobs e-mailed to you weekly; and post your resume online. Registration is required for personalization and resume features. You can also browse a list of employers to see all job openings available at each company.

CareerSite

www.careersite.com

CareerSite emphasizes a confidential approach to online job searching and recruiting. At this Web site, job seekers can create anonymous profiles of their credentials and are automatically notified when matching jobs from more than 25,000 employers are posted. You can also conduct a simple job search and respond to most employers without registering, if desired. Employers that have registered their own profiles with CareerSite have stars next to them, and you can read further information about each. One nice feature: CareerSite automatically converts your resume to Adobe Acrobat (.PDF) format to preserve its original look and feel.

FlipDog.com

www.flipdog.com

Since its debut in 2000, FlipDog has taken a unique approach. Although it contains the typical options to post your resume (with varying levels of privacy), search for jobs, and set up a personal job search agent, job listings here are indexed directly from employers' own Web sites. Search by keyword and location to pull up a list of clickable job titles, each of which directs you to the actual posting on the employer's site. Added features include career advice, articles, resources, a free semimonthly newsletter, and research information on thousands of employers. Because FlipDog's approach means that employers do not have to pay for postings, more listings can often be found here than at other sites.

HotJobs

`hotjobs.yahoo.com`

> HotJobs lets you screen out jobs posted by staffing firms if you want to deal directly with employers rather than applying through agencies. Search listings by category, company, location, or keyword, or use the advanced search for more options. You can create a HotJobs account to post your resume, set privacy options for your information, and even see statistics on how often your resume is viewed by employers. HotJobs also features job search agents that e-mail you openings matching your criteria and allows you to apply online. Be sure to browse through the career tools and news, sign up for a free e-mail newsletter, and check out online forums for discussions and networking opportunities with others in your industry. HotJobs is now owned by Yahoo!.

JobBankUSA.com

`www.jobbankusa.com`

> At JobBankUSA.com's meta-search, in addition to the jobs posted at the site itself, you can run searches in newspapers across the country or through regional job banks, other national and

international job banks, and industry-specific job banks. This makes this Web site a useful one-stop shop for searching multiple resources. Use the free Resume Builder service to create an online resume, and then, for a fee, you can use ResumeBroadcaster to have your resume e-mailed to companies that match your skills. You'll also find the typical job search agent to e-mail you matching listings, industry news, and career resources.

Monster

www.monster.com

Monster, possibly the best-known careers site on the Internet, contains all the features you would expect in a major job and resume bank. Use the First-Timers link for an overview of your options, which include registering to post your resume, have jobs e-mailed to you, signing up for e-mail newsletters, searching more than one million monthly job postings and applying online using the resume you posted in step one, and finding advice, articles, and tools in an extensive online career center. Also access Monster's related sites for senior execs, college students, relocators, and training/educational opportunities, as well as its global network of country-specific sites. Polls, message boards, and topical scheduled chats add an interactive element, and you can sign up for a "premium" account that has additional features such as career assessments, resume enhancements, and inside info for a monthly fee.

NationJob

www.nationjob.com

Search job listings by field, location, duration, educational level, and salary. Register to receive e-mail notification of new jobs matching your criteria. Research companies. Find career tools and resources. Get your degree online. Post your resume to the database. Access career articles and success stories. It's all here at NationJob's Web site.

Vault.com

`www.vault.com`

Vault.com's claim to fame lies in its "insider" information on more than 3,000 companies and 70 industries. Not enough for you? Access the "Electronic Water Cooler," online company-specific message boards where you can get the lowdown from current and former employees. Of course, you can also use traditional job bank features such as searchable job postings, an online resume service, e-mail newsletters, and e-mailed job openings. One last useful feature is an extensive resume and cover letter advice section, including the option to post your resume for viewing and critique by other Vault.com members before you send it out to employers.

Job Banks for Recent or Soon-to-Be College Graduates

The sites in this section represent a large variety of work opportunities and career advice targeted at college students and recent graduates. If you're new to the workforce, you might find your ideal entry-level job here more easily than you would at a larger job bank.

AfterCollege

www.aftercollege.com

> For college students and recent graduates, AfterCollege lets you search for entry-level jobs and internships and post your resume online to be viewed by potential employers. One nice feature for registered users is the AfterCollege agent, which allows you to store your resume on the site and e-mail it from there to any e-mail address in response to job ads—without having to copy and paste. Other neat features? The country guides offer country-specific career information about working abroad, the industry showcase highlights a number of industries, and a career advice section offers useful articles on the job search and career choice process.

The Black Collegian Online

www.black-collegian.com

> An electronic version of the magazine, Black Collegian calls itself "The Career Site for Students of Color." Here you can find job listings, post your resume (at three different privacy levels), and create personal job search agents. There are also plenty of career- and education-related articles to help provide background info for a successful job search and career. Also check out the Diversity Registry for information on employers who actively recruit college students, particularly minorities, for entry-level jobs.

CampusCareerCenter.com

www.campuscareercenter.com

> You have to register to search through the jobs and internships listed on this site. The thorough process asks for your school,

major, GPA, and work history, among other information. Apply online or send relevant job postings to your friends. Ads contain links for additional employer information and other jobs offered by that company. You'll also find career-related articles and advice, as well as a section on finding and learning about internships.

Cleveland Intern

www.clevelandintern.net

Although this site specifically connects students with internships in northeast Ohio, you can use the search engines in the Introduction to see whether your state or city sponsors a similar resource. Live in Ohio? Register for the site through your campus career center to apply for internships listed at multiple universities, and find career exploration information.

College Grad Job Hunter

http://collegegrad.com

College Grad Job Hunter is devoted to entry-level job information. It contains extensive resources for new graduates seeking to enter the job market. Sections here include career planning, resumes, cover letters, employer research, job postings, interviewing, salaries, and your new job. Also take a look at top entry-level employers, subscribe to the free job-hunting newsletter, and check out the online career forum for employment advice. The job search section is broken down into entry-level, experience required, internships, and mega job search, which allows you to search through more than 100 job banks at once.

College Recruiter

www.collegerecruiter.com

Find internships, seasonal work, and full-time and part-time opportunities. Register to sign up for the job search agent and free newsletter and to post your resume on the site. Jobs can be searched by keyword or browsed by category. You can apply for most directly online by using your posted resume or by pasting your electronic resume into an online e-mail form. In the Career

Center section, search for articles and advice on all aspects of the career search process. Other interesting and useful features include a roommate search and a database of international jobs and internships. This site is heavy on advertising, but there's a lot of good free information here as well.

JobWeb

www.jobweb.com/home.cfm

Sponsored by the National Association of Colleges and Employers, JobWeb's primary audience is recent or soon-to-be college graduates. JobWeb features an extensive, searchable employer database, as well as an online career fair, where you can find information at employer "booths" and links to individual job posting pages. Other sections include resume and interview advice, current career news, and a large library of career-related articles and career-planning information.

MonsterTRAK (formerly JOBTRAK)

www.jobtrak.com

This Monster channel, devoted to students and recent graduates, requires that your school participate in the service. You get a special password to register and search for entry-level jobs and internships. More than 1,000 colleges currently participate; a list is available online. Other perks: Get career advice and networking opportunities from alums at your own school, research companies, participate in message boards and chats, find resume advice, and browse an online career fair. You'll also find career-related articles and tools, as well as a major-to-career converter tool to help you answer that all-important question: "What can I do with my major?"

Saludos Hispanos

www.saludos.com

Focusing on career opportunities for bilingual Hispanic college graduates, Saludos Hispanos connects applicants and employers seeking to diversify their workforce. Use the career pavilion to access services for job seekers, such as listings of entry-level jobs and internships, a resume posting service, mentor profiles, guides to researching specific fields, information on career fairs, an e-mail newsletter, and additional career links. You'll also find online articles from *Saludos Hispanos* magazine.

SummerJobs.com

www.summerjobs.com

Need to find summer or seasonal employment between semesters? SummerJobs.com is the place to start. Most of these ads come from camps, resorts, amusement parks, and other places that need seasonal help. You can also view employer profiles and links to their Web sites to find out about your potential summer employer. A job resources section features information on the duties and activities you'll be responsible for in typical summer jobs at places such as parks, resorts, and cruise ships.

Other Specialized Job Banks

Specialized job banks focusing on a specific skill, aimed at specific groups, or targeted to a particular field are one of the best ways to target appropriate listings and cut through the clutter of crowded general databases. This section contains a sampling of the resources available. You can find more by browsing the clearinghouses described in the next chapter or by conducting an online search as explained in the Introduction to this book.

911hotjobs.com

www.911hotjobs.com

If careers in law enforcement or firefighting sound exciting, call on 911hotjobs.com. Search free job listings, or sign up as a paid member to search jobs from 911hotjobs.com together with those from other law enforcement Web sites. You can also order law enforcement employment and examination preparation books, sign up for a newsletter that notifies you when new positions are posted, or, for a fee, take online practice tests.

Bilingual-Jobs.com

www.bilingual-jobs.com

As you might guess from the name, Bilingual-Jobs.com offers a job bank for English-speaking bilingual professionals. Search by language, location, category, or keyword. You'll need to register to take advantage of most site features, such as resume posting, the job search agent, and applying online.

CoolWorks.com

www.coolworks.com

National parks, ski resorts, dude ranches, amusement parks, cruises... If these sound like fun places to work, get the scoop on these jobs and more at CoolWorks.com, whose motto is "Cool jobs in great places." Although many jobs are seasonal, you can also find year-round listings, as well as volunteer opportunities and internships to help build your resume. Find the latest jobs and employers at the What's New link, post your resume, or sign up to get a weekly e-mail update with the newest listings. You can even sign up for a free CoolWorks.com e-mail account here. You can browse jobs by category or search by keyword or state.

dice.com

www.dice.com

Dice.com specializes in jobs for information technology (IT) professionals. Given the nature of the IT marketplace, a number of listings here are for contract positions rather than permanent opportunities. Jobs can be searched by keyword, location, area code, type, and company and can be limited to telecommuting only or by the amount of travel required. You can also create a personalized account to have your profile available to employers (publicly or confidentially), create an online resume, and use personal search agents. You'll also find career resources targeted specifically at IT professionals, including training links and industry news.

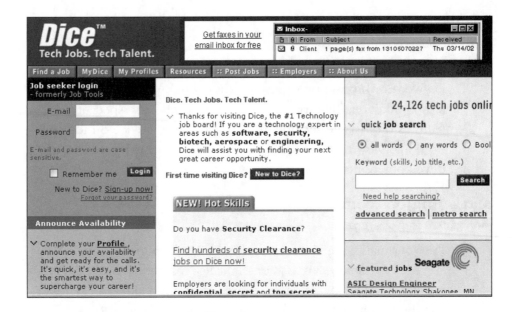

Federal Jobs Digest

www.jobsfed.com

> Want to work for the government? Federal Jobs Digest claims to list more federal vacancies than any other source. There are three options for viewing listings: free access if you post your resume, $10 for 30 days if you choose not to submit your resume, or free and anonymous to preview listings sans contact information. You also can find out about the benefits of working for the federal government, get job descriptions for federal job series, read resume advice and federal career news, or subscribe to the print version.

HealthJobsite.com

www.healthjobsite.com

> As the name implies, HealthJobsite.com focuses on careers in the booming field of health care. Job seekers can search the job listings, browse by specialty, or register to post their resume and apply online. From nursing to health administration, HealthJobsite.com includes positions in every health care category.

Lisjobs.com

www.lisjobs.com

> Librarians and information professionals can search job listings by keyword or browse by category. Not enough postings here? Access lists of additional librarian job banks by state or by specialty. Other features on this site include articles and career advice on topics from interviewing to salaries, as well as a free e-mail professional development newsletter.

MarketingJobs.com

www.marketingjobs.com

> Put your marketing skills to work with MarketingJobs.com, a Web site focusing solely on positions in sales, marketing, and advertising. Browse jobs by category, search by job function and state, or use the advanced search for more options. You can also view company profiles to find out more information before applying.

National Teacher Recruitment Clearinghouse

www.recruitingteachers.org

> The National Teacher Recruitment Clearinghouse aims to help end the teaching shortage by attracting new teachers to the profession and helping existing teachers find jobs. Find out about the teaching profession and the requirements for becoming a teacher, get tips on finding a teaching position, and learn about licensing in each state. The biggest plus of this site is its nationwide job bank portal, a meta-search clearinghouse that lets you find teacher job banks specific to your location and that lets you look for state, nationwide, or international job banks. You can also locate the Department of Education in your state.

OverseasJobs.com

www.overseasjobs.com

> International job opportunities await at OverseasJobs.com, which features searchable and geographic listings of openings worldwide. Warning: Some postings can be somewhat outdated, so be sure to check the date posted before applying. The site also includes

resources and advice targeted at those interested in working abroad, from health and safety tips to links to other international job sites, as well as a free e-mail newsletter.

Showbizjobs.com

www.showbizjobs.com

Has anyone ever told you that you ought to be in pictures? Showbizjobs.com might help you get that big break. Search by category, region, keyword, or company, or browse by date to see the most recently posted positions. Don't forget to visit the online message boards to network with others or to check the placement directory for information on agencies. Additional services, such as posting your resume and activating a Showbizjobs.com e-mail address, require paid registration.

U.S. Agency for International Development (USAID)

www.info.usaid.gov/about/employment/

For employment opportunities in humanitarian efforts worldwide, consult USAID's employment listings. Vacancy announcements are posted for foreign service new entry professionals, foreign service midlevel positions, civil service, and senior executive service.

You'll also find out about various fellows programs and access the Web site for each. Read the FAQ for answers to all your questions about working with USAID.

Regional Job Sites

If you're less than geographically mobile, or you're interested in employment in a particular region, you might want to investigate job banks specializing in positions and career advice for specific large cities, states, or geographic regions. This section contains a few examples.

CareersColorado.com

www.careerscolorado.com

> The name says it all. You search Colorado jobs and post your resume, join the e-mail list, or browse by specific large Colorado employer. An events calendar lists local career fairs and workshops, and career advice and resource links round out the site.

Chicago Jobs

www.chicagojobs.com

> Chicago Jobs provides features similar to those of the national job banks, but it focuses on positions in the Chicago area. Register to post your resume online, to get access to automatic job notification, and to subscribe to this site's mailing list. Job searches can be focused on the Loop, the greater Chicago area, or suburban areas and can be conducted by category or keyword.

Craigslist

www.craigslist.org

> Although additional craigslists are now available for selected cities across the country, the original Bay Area craigslist contains the most opportunities. Jobs are broken down by category, from writing/editing to Internet/Web development. In each category, you'll find listings organized by posting date, with the most recent first. Craigslist, however, is more than just job postings. You'll find an entire online community resource, all ad-free!

Tri-State Jobs

www.tristatejobs.com

> If you live in the Northeast, you might want to visit Tri-State Jobs for thousands of listings in New York, New Jersey, Connecticut, and Pennsylvania. You can search, post your resume, and sign up for e-mail notification of jobs matching your specifications. You also can check out info on local career fairs and find links to additional career sites and resources here.

Canadian Job Information

This section contains leads to jobs in Canada. For information on jobs in other countries, check the career clearinghouses listed in chapter 5, as well as Monster and other job banks described in this chapter, several of which provide international listings or affiliate sites. Be aware, however, that many of these postings may be only for resident citizens.

Electronic Labour Exchange

www.ele-spe.org

> The Electronic Labour Exchange takes a unique approach. Rather than posting specific openings, employers create a profile of positions they need filled. Job seekers specify their Canadian territory of residence (or outside Canada) and complete their own profile (using handy checklists), outlining their skills and the type of job they are looking for. Registered job seekers can then search for a match or advertise their completed profiles to employers.

Human Resources Development Canada: Job Bank

www.jobbank.gc.ca

> On any given day, Job Bank contains about 30,000 job postings across Canada—including a special section for student jobs. Pick your territory of residence, or choose "outside Canada" to search nationwide. Then specify your desired job title or search by keyword to retrieve postings. You'll find a link to the Canadian Citizenship and Immigration Office for information on receiving an

employment authorization if you are not a citizen or permanent resident. Job Bank also provides a number of links to other sites that are useful to Canadian job seekers.

Getting the Job

So you've used some of the job banks listed in this chapter to locate just the right position or positions. Now, what's the best way to go about applying for, and landing, the perfect job? Check out the resume and interviewing sites in the following sections for some tips on the process.

Resumes and Cover Letters

Read about electronic resumes in the Introduction to this book, and then extend your resume creation and cover letter skills by browsing the Web sites described here.

10 Minute Resume

www.10minuteresume.com

> You'll need to create a login and password to use this site—then proceed to a step-by-step walk-through of creating a basic resume. Answer the questions, fill out a couple of forms, and the site creates a formatted online resume for you and gives you the option of having it available to employers. You can also create cover letters to store on the site, convert your resume to several printable formats, e-mail or fax it to employers, or make it into a Web page. This site is a great choice if you lack confidence in your resume-creation skills.

CareerJournal.com—Resumes & Cover Letters

www.careerjournal.com/jobhunting/resumes/

> You'll find career advice from the experts at the *Wall Street Journal's* CareerJournal.com. You'll see articles on all aspects of creating and using effective resumes and cover letters, from the

drawbacks of resume-blasting services to discussions of resume-writing software packages. Read them all? Check out the other categories, including interviewing, networking, and articles on changing careers.

JobStar—Resumes & Cover Letters

`http://jobstar.org/tools/resume/`

JobStar's section on resumes and cover letters is categorized into several useful topics: What is a resume?, What is the right resume for me?, Resume samples, Resume resources on the Web, Resume tips, Electronic resume banks, About cover letters, and Sample cover letters. There's enough material here to get you started—and keep you going—as you apply for any position.

Rebecca Smith's eResumes & Resources

`www.eresumes.com`

Electronic resume expert Rebecca Smith walks you through understanding and creating the different types of electronic resumes with step-by-step tutorials and examples. She also links to a number of articles by other electronic resume-savvy writers and provides information on posting your electronic resume online, sending it through e-mail, and otherwise getting it to employers. You can also view others' Web-based resumes for inspiration or formatting ideas

The Riley Guide: Resumes & Cover Letters

`www.rileyguide.com/eresume.html`

The Riley Guide's "Preparing Your Resume for the Internet and Posting It Online" explains Internet-ready resumes, preparing a plain-text resume, rules for responding online, and placement versus privacy issues. You'll also find a link to general resume help, which provides access to a number of resume writing and electronic resume resources and tips.

Rebecca Smith's eRésumés & Resources
w w w . e r e s u m e s . c o m

Your Single Source for
Electronic Resumes and Online Networking

online since
1995

ABOUT	BOOK	eRESUMES 101	GALLERY	LINKS	PRESS
Navigation	Contents	Learn how. Or	View	Online Job	Site Author
Awards	Reviews	we can do it	Resumes	Search by	Media Kit
Disclaimer	Press	for you	on the Web	Industry	Releases

Interviewing

After your resume has landed you that all-important job interview, you can get tips and advice for interview success from the following Web sites.

Interviewing Success

www.collegegrad.com/intv/

> CollegeGrad.com is targeted at entry-level job seekers. This site includes a number of articles on interviewing successfully, aimed especially at recent college graduates who might not have much previous interviewing experience. Get ideas on questions *you* can ask during interviews, check out the list of 50 standard entry-level interview questions and prepare your answers for these commonly asked questions, learn how to have a successful phone interview, find out what to do after the interview, and more.

Job-Interview.net

www.job-interview.net

> Get prepared for tricky interview questions and situations with the reassuring advice on Job-Interview.net. Find advice and articles on

interviewing, links to other interviewing sites, sample questions and ideas on how to answer them, and learn how to turn tough questions to your advantage. Most helpful are the categorized mock interviews. You locate the one for the type of job you are applying for to see sample questions tailored to that specific position and a recommended reading list. Another great feature is a tutorial outlining how to read a job ad with an eye toward preparing for an interview for that position.

Monster: Interview Center

`http://interview.monster.com`

Start by checking out Monster's virtual interviews for a number of typical positions. Choose from among sample answers, and get evaluated on your choices. This is especially useful because it tells you why a particular answer is the best (or not the best) and gives you ideas for extending these skills into your own interviews. Elsewhere on this site, the Rehearsal section contains general articles and advice on interview success, from questions to ask the interviewer to conquering the phone interview. Stage Debut contains a number of articles discussing questions you might be asked during interviews and the best ways to answer. Critic's Review offers tips on critiquing your own interview performance, and Encore talks about second interviews, negotiation strategies, and so on.

Quintessential Careers: Job Interviewing Resources

`www.quintcareers.com/intvres.html`

This collection of useful job interviewing resources includes tutorials, articles, and tools to prepare you for any type of interview. Start with the database of sample interview questions with "excellent sample responses" to find 109 of the most commonly asked questions and good ways to answer them. Take some practice interviews to compare how your answers match up with the suggestions. Other great features here include a job interview tutorial and a quiz to test your knowledge of the subject.

CHAPTER 5

Career Clearinghouses

Your explorations of the Web sites in this book so far should have illustrated the volume and richness of the career information that's available over the Internet. Although here you'll find the "best of the best," categorized to help you quickly carry out your personal career explorations, you also might want to dig deeper and explore sites specific to your industry, new resources as they become available, and so on.

A great approach to researching career information is to get leads or referrals from the sites you use and are familiar with. You can think of this as networking on the Internet—so to speak! One advantage of this approach is that you'll start to notice that the better Web sites are mentioned frequently by a number of different sources, helping establish their reputation as quality sites and their potential value to you. One of your best bets here is to become familiar with the resources available at *career clearinghouses*.

What Is a Clearinghouse?

A clearinghouse is an index, directory, or list (sometimes called a "meta-list") of other Internet sites. Clearinghouses are good places to jump-start your research and save time, because someone has already conducted Internet searches, collected the best sites, and organized those results for you.

Clearinghouses work the same way as more-general Internet directories such as Yahoo!. Because clearinghouses are usually maintained by one (or just a few) individuals rather than by a large staff, their organization, focus, scope, and types of sites included differ. Links, however, generally are organized into separate lists, allowing you to drill down easily to your desired topic—although some (usually smaller) clearinghouses might just arrange their links in alphabetical order. Some provide search capabilities, and others are meant simply for browsing.

Any good clearinghouse provides at least a one-line description of each linked resource—and some provide more. Clearinghouse authors also like to give their stamp of approval to selected sites. These opinions often differ. You will notice, though, that the same links are often duplicated across different clearinghouses—which can give you an idea of the major sites in a particular area, or at least those that are most highly thought of by clearinghouse authors.

Although some career clearinghouse sites strive to collect a comprehensive collection of resources, others are more selective and might reflect the personal bias of their author. Use your own judgment as to which type is most useful to you as you do your own research. You will likely want to investigate more than one of these sites to find relevant resources because some list sites that do not appear on others.

The Best Clearinghouses

The following list describes some of the best clearinghouses for career and job information. Use it to identify the clearinghouses that are most useful to you, bookmark them to revisit, and then use the others to fill in when necessary.

AIRS Job Board Directory

www.airsdirectory.com/directories/job_boards/

One of the largest job board directories on the Internet, the AIRS directory lists nearly 6,500 job boards, broken down into categories by industry, international location, state and federal government, function, banks for free agents and telecommuters, and so on. Each link specifies whether the resource is free or has a fee for employers, whether it accepts resume postings, and the site's market and geographic focus. Some listings contain a Profile link that you can click to read brief information about the site before visiting. You'll also find news, forums, and other resources, although these are targeted at recruiters rather than job seekers.

Career Resource Homepage, Rensselaer Polytechnic Institute

www.careerresource.net

The award-winning Career Resource Homepage at Rensselaer Polytechnic Institute has been organized and maintained by a former student since 1994. Categories include Employers Direct, University Human Resources, Internet Job Surfer, Resumes Direct, Professional Societies and Other Organizations, Career Services at Various Universities, CyberAlumni, and Links To Other Job Resource Indexes. Each category contains an extensive list of alphabetical links.

Careers.org

www.careers.org

> Careers.org consists of more than 4,000 links to career-related
> Internet resources, organized by category. One nice feature here is
> career gems—picks for the most useful sites. A second is the link
> to an affiliated site listing job resources by U.S. state, which pro-
> vides links to a number of sites for each state. Although there's a
> lot here, be aware that the site makes no clear differentiation
> between general links and sponsored links, which try to get you to
> pay for services.

Internet Career Connection

http://iccweb.com

> Internet Connection, online on AOL since 1989, calls itself
> America's first and oldest online career guidance service. It's taken
> this time to develop searchable databases of career and employ-
> ment, internship, work-from-home, and other categorized Web
> sites. Each database listing contains a site profile you can access
> for further information before jumping to the resource itself.
> Profiles and listings are created by site visitors themselves, so some
> are more up-to-date than others. Still, this is a good starting place
> for further exploration.

Job-Hunt.org

www.job-hunt.org

> NETability Inc.–owned Job-Hunt.org contains thousands of catego-
> rized, editor-selected links to career and job-hunting sites. Its post-
> ing policy contains some job seeker-friendly information, including
> its decision not to list any sites that lack a privacy policy or that
> appear to be get-rich-quick or multilevel marketing scams. Start
> with the link on how to use Job-Hunt.org for useful advice on
> navigating the extensive resources here and on successful cyber-
> job hunting in general. Each category contains annotated lists of
> links, the best of which are indicated by smiley-face icons. Be sure
> to read the introduction to each category for ideas on other sec-
> tions to peruse and an explanation of the types of links you'll find

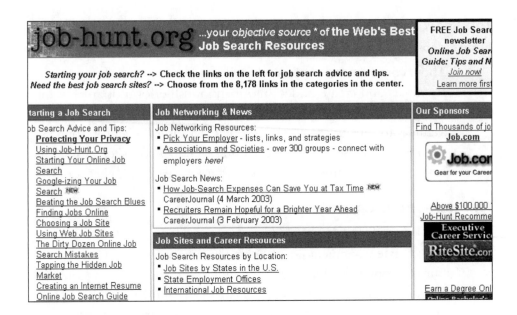

included. There's a lot here. You might want to bookmark this site and make several visits to make sure you don't miss anything!

JobHuntersBible.com

www.jobhuntersbible.com

Richard Bolles created this Web site as a companion resource to his perennially popular book, *What Color Is Your Parachute?* Links here are divided into two major categories: The Net Guide, which contains a collection of information and resources for Internet job hunting, and The Parachute Library, a collection of career-related articles written by Bolles and other contributors. He provides useful insight into and advice on using the sections of The Net Guide in the form of Fairy Godmother Reports, which explain the realities of resume posting, career assessments, and other popular Internet career activities. Also find out about the latest edition of his book, including ordering information.

Job Searching Directory: About.com

http://jobsearch.about.com/cs/allsubjects/

About.com features experts who whose job it is to pick the best resources and create added information in the form of articles and annotations. The Job Searching Directory is compiled by just such a guide and includes categorized links to career-related resources from job databases to resume writing to relocation sites. Additional features include articles, forums, and a job searching chat room.

Quintessential Careers

www.quintcareers.com

For an extensive meta-list of links, visit Quintessential Careers. Current content will keep you coming back; the front page alone features an article of the week, a career tip and tool of the day, and a featured-career site. New visitors should try the site tour, which explains the best ways to use the site (depending on what you're looking for!). It also contains a quick-find drop-down menu, a link to a "portal" page, and a link to site-search, giving you several different ways to access resources. Also sign up for a free newsletter or check out the New Additions page to see what's been added recently.

The Riley Guide: Employment Opportunities and Job Resources on the Internet

www.rileyguide.com

One of the best and most comprehensive career and job information clearinghouses on the Internet, The Riley Guide has been online since 1994. Its simple, ad-free design might be short on flashiness, but the site is deep in content, and the What's New page provides weekly updates on what's been added. Pick from the major categories listed on the front page, or use the A-Z index for an alphabetical list of the thousands of resources here. Each major category is broken down into subcategories, and each of these provides suggestions on other related subcategories to try. The site was created and is maintained by Margaret Riley Dikel, author of *The Guide to Internet Job Searching*.

Workindex.com

`www.workindex.com`

Workindex.com calls itself the gateway to human resources solutions. It contains more than 4,000 Web site links for HR professionals. Luckily, many of these are also tremendously useful to job seekers as well! Sites are listed by category, and you can read a brief description of each before visiting. You can also conduct a keyword search if you don't find what you're looking for through the directory index.

Researching Employer and Labor Market Information

Any organized job seeker will want to research potential employers before applying for a job or in preparation for an interview. A number of resources help you find enough information on companies to help you make an informed decision—or an informed impression! Additional employer information can be found through the job banks listed in chapter 4, as well as the career clearinghouses described in chapter 5.

Other information you can research online includes labor market information. This data tells you a lot about the changing economy, which occupations are changing or growing, and what employees might expect in the near future—all good background material to have before making a career move or relocating for a job. Entrepreneurs can research wage information when planning how they will staff their new businesses or look into state personal income and industry information when deciding where to locate. Union officials can see inflation rates and other economic information before negotiating contracts.

For more detailed information on related resources, programs, and data for your state, see the list of state employment/workforce-development agencies listed in chapter 4. Also note that the state-based career information systems mentioned in chapter 3 base their projections on labor market information. The agencies and organizations in this chapter use the power of the Internet to make useful and user-friendly labor market information available to everyone.

Researching Employers

Here are some general sites for researching employers online. Remember that one of the best sources of information on a company can be its own Web site. Search for employer Web sites by using the search engines and strategies discussed in the Introduction.

CorporateInformation.com

`www.corporateinformation.com`

> You have to register to use this company research site, but basic registration is free. It includes research companies, industries, states, and more. Type a company's name into the search box on the front page to find information on specific companies, which includes a brief analysis from this site as well as links to articles and company profiles from other Web sites. Although much information is targeted at investors, you'll find useful background material for your job hunt as well. You can also pick a state to find information on every company the site covers in that state or use an alphabetical list to browse corporations. This site is best for information on large companies.

Google News

`http://news.google.com`

> Search and browse 4,000 news sources from leading search engine Google. Find the most up-to-date news stories on specific companies, or simply pick the Business section to read current articles. This is a great way to keep current on industries and specific companies. You can find out what's going on before applying or in preparation for an interview. Articles stay in the index for 30 days.

Hoover's Online

`www.hoovers.com`

> Hoover's Online provides some employer information for free and more for a fee. Search by company name, ticker symbol, keyword, and so on to access company capsules, Web sites, stock information, basic financials, and news. Also read featured business news stories on the front page and register for e-mail news alerts on the

businesses and industries that interest you, as well as for a number of free newsletters.

SuperPages

`www.superpages.com/business/`

Verizon's SuperPages is an electronic yellow pages—with a twist. Search for U.S. businesses by name and location, or browse by category. Each listing contains contact information as well as a Web site link when available, plus a map and driving directions. Register to create your own directory of saved listings. You can also search for businesses by geographic location if you're looking for potential places to apply in your area.

Thomas Register

`www.thomasregister.com`

Thomas Register takes its print manuals online, allowing registered users to search for manufacturers and companies and view their catalogs and Web sites. Check out the demo to see how searching works and what information is included in manufacturer listings. Although the site is meant largely for locating suppliers, it's a useful way for job seekers to locate companies in their industry as well.

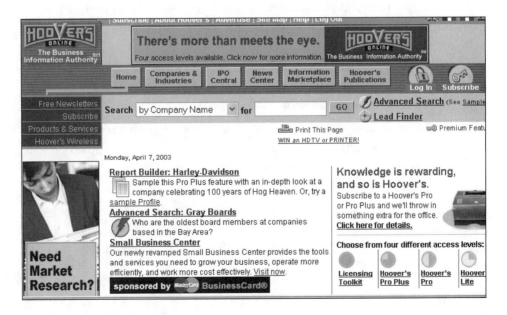

Company Research Tutorials

For tips and instructions on researching employers, check out these Web sites.

Industry Research Desk

www.virtualpet.com/industry/

> This 19-step process walks you through researching a specific company or a specific industry—helpful background info to have before going for that interview or applying for that position. There are a ton of links to useful resources included among the steps, so take some time to explore. You'll also find ideas on print resources that can also be useful; you can find many of these at your local public or college library.

Researching Companies Online

http://home.sprintmail.com/~debflanagan/

> This step-by-step tutorial from Internet trainer Debbie Flanagan contains surefire tips for locating free company and industry information on the Web. Topics here include locating company home pages, monitoring company news, learning about an industry, identifying international business resources, and researching non-profit organizations. Each topic includes useful links and instructions, and you can also access her Web Search Strategies tutorial from here.

Riley Guide: Using the Internet to Do Job Search Research

www.rileyguide.com/jsresearch.html

> The venerable Riley Guide provides another useful resource for your job search, this one focusing on researching employers on the Internet. The first section provides general tips on doing effective Internet research, and the second gives specific advice on finding company information. This step-by-step tutorial shows you how to do research on all aspects of your job search, and it links to a number of sites for additional information and ideas.

Company Rankings

A number of magazines and Web sites have begun preparing rankings of the "best" companies to work for, many updated yearly. Like the *U.S. News & World Report* college rankings mentioned in chapter 1, you'll want to take these with a grain of salt, but they can give you an idea of well-regarded companies where you might want to try to get your foot in the door.

50 Best Companies to Work for in Canada

was.hewitt.com/hewitt/worldwide/canada/articles/best_companies/
lists/the_list_2003.htm

> *Report on Business* magazine's Hewitt-compiled annual list of Canada's top 50 employers. For links to other top Canadian companies, such as the top 50 tech companies and 50 largest employers, see R.O.B.'s Web site at www.theglobeandmail.com/robmagazine/.

100 Best Companies for Working Mothers

www.workingwoman.com/100best.shtml

> *Working Mother's* annual list of the 100 best companies for working mothers provides handy links to the Web site of each so that you can find further information. The top ten list online includes brief information on why each was selected, and Best in Class lists the winner in each of six work/life categories. You'll have to get your hands on the print issue to see full company profiles; order online or check your local library.

BestJobsUSA.com's Employers of Choice 500

www.employersofchoice.com

> BestJobsUSA.com uses a number of other surveys and public information to compile its own annual list of the best 500 companies to work for. Then it provides lists of the top 50 in a number of sub-categories (diversity, education, energy, finance, healthcare, IT, pharmaceutical, and sales). Best of the Best links to rankings from other sites and magazines.

Computerworld: The Best Places to Work in IT

www.computerworld.com/bestplaces2002/

> A number of places provide industry-specific rankings, which can be useful in researching the best companies to work for after you have settled on a particular field. *Computerworld's* list of the best places to work in IT annually ranks the best information technology employers, both in the U.S. and globally. You can also read related articles and learn about the methodology behind the rankings.

Fortune: 100 Best Companies to Work For

www.fortune.com/fortune/bestcompanies/

> *Fortune* initiated the whole company-ranking trend, and it continues to create its annual list of the 100 best companies to work for. Be sure to read the related articles on finding the best company for you, how companies satisfy workers, and other related topics. This site also links to other rankings, including the 100 fastest-growing companies, the small-business 100, and the 50 best for minorities.

Researching Labor Market Information

Labor market information includes data about workers, industries, employers, wages, and trends—much of which is made freely available online by government and other sources.

Government Sources

Most key national labor market indicators are developed by federal and state agencies. Use the government sources in this section to research industry employment estimates and projections, occupational data, labor force statistics, unemployment rates, employment hours and earnings, the consumer price index, demographic and socioeconomic data, population estimates and projections, business cycle indicators, and more. In addition, the Web sites described in this section provide information on federal programs and initiatives that affect the U.S. workforce, such as the Workforce Investment Act of 1998. To view many of the files on these sites, you need Adobe Acrobat Reader, which is available for free from the Adobe Web site at www.adobe.com/products/acrobat/readstep2.html.

Bureau of Economic Analysis (BEA)

www.bea.gov

> The BEA, an agency of the U.S. Department of Commerce, is a major resource for economic, business, and labor market data. Find summary data and articles broken down by national, international, industry, and regional (state and local) categories. Current news releases and a What's New page show you data that has been recently updated, or click the Using Our Site link for hints and tips on navigation and opening files. This is your source of information on the GDP (Gross Domestic Product) and GDP by industry, our international trade deficit, personal income by state and county, and much more. You'll also find articles that summarize and explain all this data.

Bureau of Labor Statistics (BLS)

www.bls.gov

> The U.S. BLS is a one-stop shop for labor market information and statistics. Start with the handy "latest numbers" chart to find out the current unemployment rate, consumer price index, average hourly earnings, and other useful numbers for your research. You can also access regional BLS offices for information targeted to your area to get statistics on the regional economy by state and metropolitan area (such as the current unemployment rate in your city or employment statistics by industry). This site is searchable and contains an A–Z index to help you find needed information. Or you can drill down through the categories listed on the front page (including demographics, occupations, wages, earnings, benefits, and more) to locate your specific topic of interest.

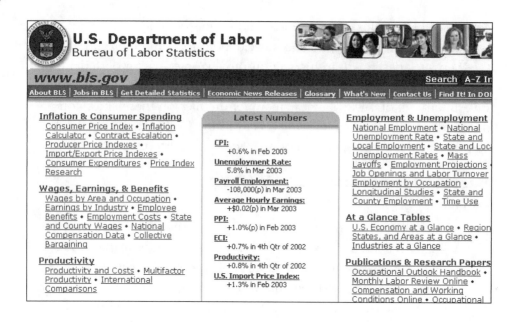

Census Bureau

www.census.gov

The Census Bureau, another agency of the U.S. Department of
Commerce, should be your first stop for demographic and socioeconomic data. Categories here include current U.S. Census data,
people, business, geography, news, and special topics. From the
front page you can also view current U.S. and world population
clocks and a link to state and county quick facts and the latest
economic indicators. You'll definitely want to check out the
American FactFinder, an interactive database tool that allows you
to easily access Census 2000 information—even down to census
block by street address! Also access income and poverty statistics,
population projections, housing information, the latest economic
census data by industry and state, and more. Use the subjects A-Z
guide or the site search tool if you can't locate your needed info
by category.

Census Bureau: Statistical Abstract of the United States

www.census.gov/statab/www/

The Statistical Abstract of the United States provides a wealth of Census Bureau information, broken down into handy tables for easy viewing and comparison. What can you find here? Employment and unemployment statistics, broken down by age, sex, race, metropolitan area, and any other measurement the Census Bureau tracks, or state rankings by population, crime rate, unemployment rate, and more. The Statistical Abstract is the resource of choice for the most useful U.S. social and economic data.

Department of Labor

www.dol.gov

The U.S. Department of Labor's Web site gives you quick access to programs such as America's Job Bank and ACINet, the Job Corps, America's Learning eXchange, and more. You'll also find an employment law guide that helps you understand your rights in the workplace, including information on such major initiatives as the Family and Medical Leave Act, minimum wage, whistleblower protection, and occupational safety and health regulations. Starting a small business? Information abounds here for you as well. You can download required workplace posters, research labor statistics and data, access the Office of Small Business Programs, and find out about employment law as it pertains to employers. You can use the standard search and A-Z index tools to quickly locate specific info.

Department of Labor Employment and Training Administration (ETA)

www.doleta.gov

The ETA's mission is "Directing business, adults, youth, dislocated workers, and workforce professionals to training and employment services," and its site provides handy access to and information about such services. Some of the resources here will be familiar to you from previous chapters, such as O*NET, apprenticeship programs, and so on. The What's New section on the front page lists new initiatives, guidelines, and programs you might want to stay aware of, and the Find It! link provides quick links to information by topic or audience. Major sections for business, research, and job seekers help you identify the information most relevant to your needs.

FedStats

www.fedstats.gov

FedStats is the government's portal to statistics from more than 100 federal agencies. You can access the data here in a number of ways, from an A-Z index to information by state to a search across all these agencies' Web sites at once. You'll also find an alphabetical list of agencies, with a brief description of the mission and the key types of statistics compiled by each. If you don't know which agency keeps the statistics you need, this is a great place to begin.

Workforce Development Organizations

The organizations described in this section play a role in programs dealing with workforce development. Their sites serve as another resource for researching labor market information as well as information on local and national workforce development programs.

National Alliance of Business (NAB)

www.nab.com

NAB's purpose is to leverage business leadership and influence into improving education and student achievement to promote workforce development through education and lifelong learning. Find out here about membership benefits, including publications, information on workforce trends, and conference discounts—which might be of special interest to you if you run or are planning your own small business. Also review information on NAB's initiatives, read reports on education and workforce development, and order low-cost or free brochures.

National Association of Workforce Boards (NAWB)

www.nawb.org

> NAWB (formerly NAPIC) represents the interests of the nation's workforce investment boards: local employer-led partnerships aimed at developing the workforce through local education, job training, and employment programs. Boards are comprised of volunteer businesspeople and are intended to provide a supply of well-trained employees. On this site, print free copies of publications, find information on sponsored projects such as job openings with Americorps*VISTA, learn about legislative actions, and find a number of other workforce development links.

Workforce ATM

www.icesa.org

> Workforce ATM is a service of the National Association of State Work Force Agencies, the national organization of state administrators of unemployment insurance, employment and training services, and labor market information programs. This Web site helps track information on related initiatives, providing links to each state's workforce development and employer services agencies, and featured news and headlines on topics from dislocated workers to veterans' services. Although much of the information here is for members only, the public sections of the site provide a great way to keep up with workforce development news and information.

Workforce Excellence Network

www.workforce-excellence.net

> The Workforce Excellence Network is an initiative of the National Association of State Workforce Board Chairs and the National Association of Workforce Boards to build the capacity and enhance the performance of the nation's public workforce development system. The resources here are aimed fairly specifically at workforce boards themselves, but searchable databases of workforce and leadership resources provide some interesting links and information.

CHAPTER 7

Military Careers

The U.S. Military is one of the country's largest employers, including service members on full-time active duty, part-time reservists, and National Guard members. Each year, the military hires over 365,000 new enlisted and officer personnel. Find out about your many options by exploring the sites in this chapter, which explain military recruiting, the different branches, service academies, reserves and the National Guard, and civilian job opportunities. You'll also find sites that will be helpful as you make the jump back to civilian employment after your military career.

In addition to helping you learn whether the military is for you, the information on these sites can get you up to speed before you sit down to talk to a recruiter. Doing your research always pays off!

Beyond the learning opportunities serving in the military itself offers, the U.S. Military also sponsors a number of lifelong and distance-learning options for current and retired service members. You can find information on these programs in chapter 2.

General Information

The ASVAB Program for Exploring Careers

http://asvabprogram.com

> The ASVAB's (Armed Services Vocational Aptitude Battery) main purpose is to show students and potential recruits where their aptitudes and abilities lie, helping them make the best military, educational, and career choices. All new recruits must take the exam in order to determine which military careers they are eligible for. This comprehensive site supports the ASVAB Program for Exploring Careers, which is used in many schools to help students make these choices. Find information on skills, interest areas, work values, education options, career exploration, and career planning, and see sample ASVAB questions.

Military Career Guide Online

www.militarycareers.com

> Details on 152 military occupations are color-coded at the top of each page—blue for enlisted, red for officer positions. Search to find occupations that meet your interests, or browse by category. Each description includes information on areas such as duties, work environment, physical demands, and education required. You can also use the Introduction to the Armed Forces section to find out about each service branch, including becoming an officer, enlistment, and where to find additional information.

Military.com Recruiting

www.military.com/Recruiting/Home/

> Get all the insider tips on joining the military in a no-pressure environment. Here are just some of the things you can do at this site: Sign up to receive free e-mail newsletters on military jobs or recruiting news, get free ASVAB test preparation info, including a sample test, and search through more than 4,100 military jobs to find those that match your interests. You can also talk to other

potential recruits and get advice and information on online discussion boards. Start with Learn From the Insider to get tips on dealing with recruiters, understanding the commitment you make when you join the military—and getting through boot camp!

My Future

www.myfuture.com

Here you can sign up to receive more information on branches of the service that interest you, watch a five-part video about the Defense Information School, take work interest and personality quizzes, and find out about military education funding. But the meat of this site lies in the Military Opportunities section. Check out information on all the military has to offer, including photo tours of the different branches, military college programs, and training. Start with common military questions and learn how to join, the benefits of joining the military, and useful questions to ask your recruiter.

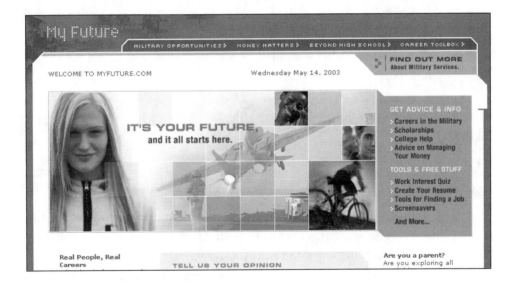

U.S. Military Branches of Service

Air Force

Air Force Link/Your Career

www.af.mil/careers.asp

Information on careers for civilians, enlisted personnel, officers, and retirees can be found here. Look through current employment opportunities and find out about pay scales, promotions, retirement pay, and all the other details of an Air Force career. This site also includes links to many other Air Force sites, as well as news and information for those contemplating the Air Force as a career.

U.S. Air Force

www.airforce.com

This official recruiting Web site for the U.S. Air Force requires the latest Macromedia Flash and other multimedia plugins to "Cross Into the Blue" and capture the excitement of an Air Force career. Browse through career fields by category to find the one that's right for you, and find out about all the benefits of an Air Force career. You can also sign up to receive more information, or even chat online with an advisor!

Army

U.S. Army

www.army.mil

The official U.S. Army site includes tons of information for anyone interested in learning how to be "An Army of One." You could spend hours browsing through the news and links here, or search for the specific information you need. Pick the Career Management link to find out about Army careers, including enlisted, officer, and civilian opportunities.

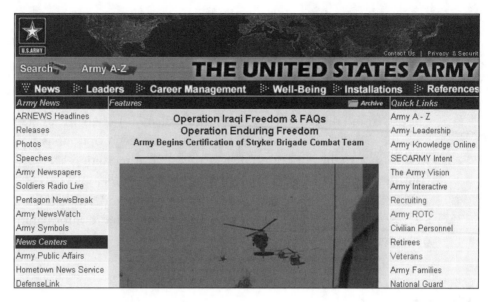

U.S. Army Recruiting

www.goarmy.com

The official U.S. Army recruiting portal tries to capture online the thrill of an Army career. Army 101 explains step-by-step the process and benefits of joining the Army, and the Jobs section explains different career options. The Basic Training section gives you a realistic picture of what you can expect by showing videos of actual recruits going through training exercises. Convinced the Army is right for you? Chat with a recruiter online, or send for additional information.

Coast Guard

U.S. Coast Guard

www.uscg.mil

Part of the U.S. Department of Transportation, the Coast Guard provides links on its official site to news and events, services, units and locations, recruiting, jobs, facts, photos, history, and more. Its motto is "Semper Paratus—Always Ready!" This site provides all the details you need about this service branch.

U.S. Coast Guard Recruiting

`www.gocoastguard.com`

Choose from enlisted, officer, reserve, auxiliary, or civilian careers with the Coast Guard, and find information on each option, as well as scholarship opportunities, at this official recruiting site. On your first visit, start with the recruiting FAQ, which should have answers to your every question about joining up and serving in the Coast Guard. You can also sign up to receive more information or locate a recruiter near you.

Marines

Marines.com

`www.marines.com`

This official recruiting site for the U.S. Marines contains information targeted at college students, high school students, college graduates, and community college students. Choose from Flash or HTML tours of the Marines. When you're finished, click Get More Information for an online form.

U.S. Marine Corps

`www.usmc.mil`

The official Marine Corps Web site covers all things Marine, from the band to news to history, video, and images of the Corps. Visit the site map link for a quick overview of all the information available here, search for a desired topic, or simply browse the main page for links to current stories and info.

Navy

U.S. Navy

www.navy.mil

> Welcome aboard the official U.S. Navy Web site, your one-stop shop for information on everything from careers to ships. The site index and site search are your doorways to finding all the facts you need, or click Got a Question? for FAQs and answers. A special What's New page lets you find out what has been added since your last visit.

U.S. Navy Opportunities

www.navyjobs.com

> "Accelerate Your Life" at the Navy's official recruitment site. Store and organize information in your personal Navy locker, which you can revisit at any time. Mark your calendar for the Navy's monthly live Webcasts, where you can get your questions answered by experts, or click Have a Question? to explore FAQs. This site covers Navy careers and benefits, educational opportunities, and what to expect from either officer or enlisted paths.

U.S. Service Academies

The service academies give you a four-year college education while preparing you for a career as an officer in one of the armed forces. Strict admissions guidelines consider such factors as U.S. citizenship (with certain exceptions), academic performance, standardized test scores, extracurricular activities, athletic ability, age, marital status, and moral character. All but the Coast Guard Academy require that you be nominated by a member of Congress or another qualified nominator.

U.S. Air Force Academy

www.usafa.af.mil

> This official site of the U.S. Air Force Academy in Colorado Springs, Colorado offers a wealth of information on all aspects of student life, academics, and programs. Highlights include a QuickTime virtual tour, admissions info for prospective students, an online application form, and a downloadable .pdf version of the current Academy catalog. "After the Academy" explains the opportunities an Academy education leads to.

U.S. Coast Guard Academy

www.cga.edu

> Learn all about the Connecticut-based Coast Guard Academy at its official Web site. The Prospective Cadet link leads to quick information on the Academy, from an overview to an online application form to FAQs. News, history, candidate profiles, and information on cadet life and academics can help you evaluate the Academy's programs.

U.S. Merchant Marine Academy

www.usmma.edu

> Find out what it takes to be admitted to the U.S. Merchant Marine Academy in Kings Point, New York by browsing the downloadable .pdf catalog, reading admissions requirements, or filling out an online admissions form. Other helpful links describe midshipman life, academic life, majors, and career services.

U.S. Military Academy (West Point)

www.usma.edu

> Perhaps the most famous of these academies, West Point celebrated its bicentennial in 2002. Join the celebration with online videos and historic photos. Start with About the Academy to explore its programs, including academic, physical, military, and moral-ethical components. Admissions information includes info on the West Point Prep military academy for prospective Academy candidates. A site search and FAQs help you drill down to the information you need.

U.S. Naval Academy

www.nadn.navy.mil

> This official site for the U.S. Naval Academy in Annapolis, Maryland, includes a site index and a search feature for locating quick information. Or you can browse through the announcements and links listed here. Admissions information includes extensive suggestions and guidelines, as well as a description of the Academy's summer seminar, which allows high school seniors to visit the campus for a week to experience all aspects of Academy life before applying.

National Guard

The oldest component of the U.S. Armed Forces, the National Guard celebrates 367 years in 2003. Its dual mission is to support the armed forces in times of war and to maintain order at a state level during emergencies. Find out about the different branches and about full- and part-time soldier and civilian opportunities at the sites described here.

Air National Guard

Air National Guard (ANG)

www.ang.af.mil

> The official site of the Air National Guard includes recruiting info, the history of the ANG, career opportunities, and links to ANG units across the country. Highlights include extensive historical information, including This Month in History, and the latest news about the ANG. Use the FAQs or search the site to quickly locate information.

Air National Guard Recruitment

www.goang.com

> Explore recruiting information and career opportunities with the Air National Guard, request information from your local recruiter,

and find out the benefits that even a part-time Air National Guard career can bring. You can also search for open positions by state or keyword, get the real scoop on basic training, and take a virtual tour. Getting tired? Enjoy an air battle or parachute mission game in the online arcade.

Army National Guard

Army National Guard

www.arng.ngb.army.mil

The Army National Guard site features extensive information, most easily accessed from the site map, FAQs, or search tools. Read current news or explore the Guard's history and mission. Use the unit search tool to find Guard units in each state, and read about the Guard's dual federal and state missions.

Army National Guard Recruitment

www.1800goguard.com

The official Army National Guard online recruiting center includes information for students and graduates, veterans, and medical professionals. You can request further information or browse the News page for current stories and to sign up for e-mail updates. Check out the Jobs section to see what civilian opportunities your Guard career can prepare you for; browse multimedia options for video, audio, and images; or play military and puzzle games online. You can also chat in real time with other site visitors.

The Reserves

The Armed Forces Reserves are military personnel who are not normally on full-time active duty but who are trained and equipped to be mobilized during a war or national crisis. High school graduates can apply to ROTC (Reserve Officer Training Corps) programs to earn a college education while also receiving officer training in their military branch.

Air Force

U.S. Air Force Reserve

www.afreserve.com

> The Air Force Reserve site features information on several categories of service, eligibility requirements, basic training, and Reserve culture, and on the many benefits—and responsibilities—of joining. Browse through News and Events to find out what's going on, request more information online, or locate a recruiter in your area to find out more.

U.S. Air Force Reserve Officer Training Corps (ROTC)

www.afrotc.com

> More than 900 U.S. colleges and universities participate in the Air Force ROTC program. Get information on the program, read about admissions standards and requirements, apply online for a scholarship, or request more information through the online form. Stories of individual cadets give you an idea of what the program is really like, and you can explore Air Force careers to see what opportunities await you after graduation.

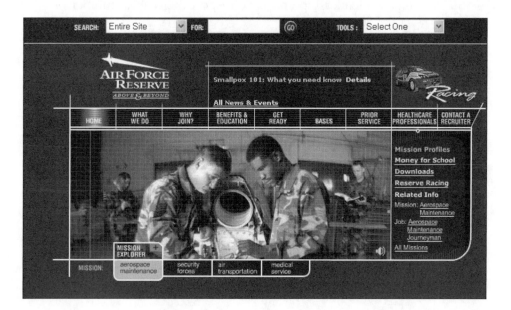

Army

U.S. Army Reserve

www.army.mil/usar/

> Visitors to this site can read FAQs; find out about jobs, benefits, and careers; and follow reservists through basic training and read their profiles online. You can also view the latest *Army Reserve* magazine in .pdf format to find out the latest, or browse through news stories and multimedia galleries to view the current state and history of the Army Reserve. Under Resources, you can thoroughly explore benefits and recruitment details and find out about the different Reserve programs offered.

U.S. Army Reserve Officer Training Corps (ROTC)

www-rotc.monroe.army.mil

> The official Army ROTC site provides all the information you need on the program, from scholarship information and links to participating schools to a useful FAQ. You can download current forms, apply online, and find out current policies. High school students might want to check out the section on Junior ROTC, a program that teaches leadership and civic responsibility in a number of schools.

Coast Guard

U.S. Coast Guard Reserve

www.uscg.mil/reserve/

> Find out all about the reservist categories and benefits of the U.S. Coast Guard Reserve. If you still have questions, fill out an information request form, or locate your local recruiting office. You can also read the current issue of the *U.S. Coast Guard Reservist* for the latest news. Current reservists can post their skills and information in the Reserve availability pool, which is accessible only from Coast Guard workstations.

Navy

U.S. Naval Reserve

www.navy-reserve-jobs.com

> To be sure you don't miss any of the information on this site, start with the site map to get an overview of the categories covered, which include enlisted and officer opportunities, benefits, application information, and recruiting information. You can also check the events calendar for upcoming recruiting events, browse FAQs, or fill out a form to request more information—even apply online!

U.S. Naval Reserve Officer Training Corps (NROTC)

https://www.nrotc.navy.mil

> The official Navy ROTC site covers the requirements, benefits, and obligations of the program, which qualifies participants for either the Navy or Marine Corps Reserves. More information is available from recruiters from either branch. Check the state-by-state list of affiliated colleges to find a program near you, or e-mail or call for more details. If you have already applied, you can check the status of your scholarship application online.

Civilian Opportunities in the Military

Soldiers are not the only contributors to the effectiveness of our Armed Forces. Find out here about opportunities for civilians to serve while earning a living by pursuing a career as a military employee.

Air Force Directorate of Civilian Career Management

www.afpc.randolph.af.mil/cp/

> Although this site largely describes training programs and career opportunities for current civilian Air Force employees, it's a great place to get a glimpse of civilian Air Force careers. Intrigued? Visit USAJOBS at www.usajobs.opm.gov to apply for federal employment and find more information.

Army Civilian Personnel Online

`http://cpol.army.mil`

> Like the Air Force site just described, the Army Civilian Personnel site is aimed largely at existing employees, but it can give you an idea of the types of jobs and training opportunities available. Create an online resume and view the status of your job applications online, and browse through open opportunities by announcement number, state or country, or broad category.

Department of the Navy Civilian Human Resources

`www.donhr.navy.mil`

> Join some 82,000 other civilian employees by pursuing a career with the U.S. Navy or Marine Corps. Start by browsing the extensive job openings on this site, which can be searched by title or geographic region. Use the resume builder to create and save your resume, and then apply online by clicking the link at the end of each job description. Before applying, you might want to examine information on common hiring categories to see which you fall into, as well as the links to pay and benefits information. Current employees can find out about training and career development opportunities and read news or bulletins affecting their working environment.

U.S. Coast Guard Civilian Personnel

`www.uscg.mil/hq/cgpc/cpm/home/geninfo.htm`

> Find a diverse list of current job openings with the U.S. Coast Guard, and use the automated application system to apply for each position. Pay scale information is useful before you apply, and current employees will find an online employee newsletter, benefits information, a list of telecommuting coordinators, and other helpful links.

Post-Military Careers

In addition to the military and government-funded employment assistance programs that exist to help active military personnel make the jump back into civilian employment, other organizations have also stepped into the gap to help connect veterans with employers.

Corporate Gray Online

www.greentogray.com

> Corporate Gray online exists for one purpose: to provide free military transition services for veterans. Post your resume to apply online with hundreds of "military-friendly" companies, or make an in-person visit to one of the military job fairs Corporate Gray sponsors across the U.S. You can also sign up to have new job listings matching your criteria sent automatically to your e-mail box. If that's not enough, you can find training and educational opportunities for veterans, as well as helpful tips on relocation, links to sites for doing company research, FAQs, and other job search resources. Every separating or retiring service member receives a copy of one of Corporate Gray's publications, which are supplemented with the information here.

Department of Defense (DoD) Transportal

www.dodtransportal.org

> This portal for transitioning military provides information on DoD transition assistance services, including contact information for the different branches, information on relocation assistance, and so on. You can also find a link to Operation Transition, a job bulletin board containing thousands of ads and other information for separating or retiring military personnel, as well as to other job banks of particular interest to former military personnel.

Department of Labor Veterans' Employment and Training Service

http://umet-vets.dol.gov

> The Department of Labor sponsors this site to help vets obtain the licenses and certifications they need to put their military

experience to work in the civilian workforce. Start with the section on transitioning to civilian careers to find out how to get credentialed in the occupations that most closely match common military specialties, get information on federal jobs that veterans might be a good match for, and read a FAQ explaining everything you need to know about credentialing.

TAOnline.com

www.taonline.com

TAOnline.com provides a wealth of transition assistance for separating or retiring military personnel, veterans, reservists, family members, and DoD civilian employees. Search job ads using multiple search criteria or simply browse all available positions, read specific transitioning military career advice and articles, or check out the transition information center for a number of useful links. You can also sign up for an electronic newsletter that provides information on job-seeker services for the military community.

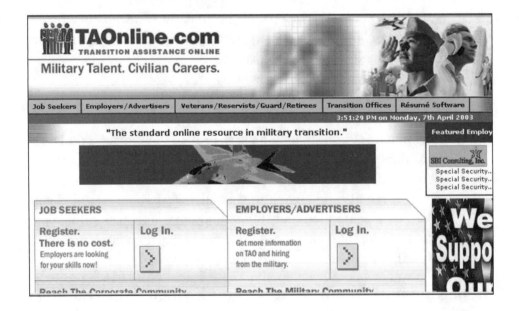

VetJobs.com

`www.vetjobs.com`

VetJobs.com is sponsored by the U.S. Veterans of Foreign Wars (VFW) to help vets understand how to approach the civilian job market and help employers appreciate veterans' skills and capabilities. Search the job database or post your resume online to let potential employers find you. You can also subscribe to a free monthly e-mail newsletter to get tips on using the site and on making the transition. Also check out resources and organizations for additional support, or see the employment assistance category for tips on interviewing and job hunting in the civilian sector.

Self-Employment and Small Business

Thinking about self-employment? You're far from alone. Working for yourself has become the new American dream. According to the U.S. Small Business Administration (SBA), there are nearly 25 million small businesses in the U.S., and some 7% of the workforce is self-employed through their own small business.

Although the SBA's definition of "small" might differ from yours, including businesses with several hundred employees and several million dollars in annual sales, it addresses the needs of millions of sole proprietorships, partnerships, and other one-person, two-person, or several-person shows.

Many self-employed people start the process by working as a free agent or contractor and then extend the concept to create their own business. (For more on free agency, see chapter 9.) Whether you work from home as a one-person band or create a business that grows to employ tens (or hundreds!) of people, owning your own business puts you in control of your own employment—and of much, much more.

Before investing your money in self-employment, it is always a good idea to first invest your time and thoroughly research your ideas. The Web sites in this chapter provide you with convenient, quality information to help you make informed decisions.

Government Resources for Small Business

The federal Web sites in this section help you get started with owning and running your own business. However, be sure to check with state and local agencies for business regulations and requirements in your location. (Locate your state's Web site at www.state.*XX*.us, where *XX* is your state's two-letter postal abbreviation, and then look for a "business" link.)

Internal Revenue Service (IRS)

www.irs.gov/businesses/small/

> Taxes are probably the last thing you want to think about when striking out on your own or beginning a business, but your tax situation is bound to change dramatically when you do take that step. The IRS's business center includes a section devoted to small businesses and the self-employed. It should be one of your first stops as you begin to plan. Find downloadable forms and publications, order free CD-ROMs and tax-year calendars, browse small business news stories and tax-law changes, and more. Take advantage of anything the IRS provides you for free!

SCORE: Counselors to America's Small Business

www.score.org

> The 10,500 members of SCORE, the Service Corps of Retired Executives, provide free and confidential e-mail and in-person small business mentoring and advice. Use this site to locate an office near you or to search for an e-mail counselor whose skills match your needs. You'll also find success stories, articles, information and links on starting a business, answers to the top ten small business questions received by SCORE counselors, and free e-mail newsletters on resources and entrepreneurial issues.

U.S. Business Advisor

www.business.gov

> Visit the U.S. Business Advisor for one-stop access to federal information and services. Because more than 60 federal organizations

assist or regulate U.S. businesses, this site can save you a lot of time. The searchable FAQs include information from all these organizations. You can also pick one of the subject areas from the front page to drill down to your topic of interest, or visit the well-organized site map to explore further. Everything from paying taxes and financing a business to selling your goods and services to the government is covered here.

U.S. Small Business Administration (SBA)

`www.sbaonline.sba.gov`

Make the U.S. SBA one of your first stops on the road to self-employment—and don't forget to come back and visit again along the way. The Starting Your Business link includes a wealth of useful information as well as an online Small Business Startup Kit (which you can also order in print from your local SBA office). Locate your local office, browse FAQs for answers to the questions aspiring small business owners most often ask, and find detailed information on common tasks such as creating your business plan. Other features include information on small business laws and regulations, help in financing your business, and free online self-paced courses for entrepreneurs.

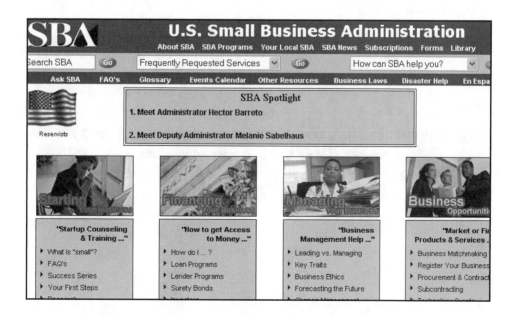

Small Business Solutions

From the time you begin thinking about starting your own business, you'll need to market your work to others, research your ideas, stay on the right side of both the law and the IRS, and judge your own entrepreneurial bent. The Web sites in this section show you how, including information useful for beginning entrepreneurs (on writing business plans, registering your Internet domain, and starting your own business) as well as more-established small business owners.

About.com: Small Business Information

`http://sbinformation.about.com`

> Although About.com is unfortunately heavy on pop-ups and other intrusive advertising, this site offers extensive information for small business owners (and aspiring owners). Subscribe to a free e-mail newsletter, join other small businesspeople for online chats, read featured articles, or select a topic of interest from the subject links here. Each subject link contains a number of links to useful sites on the topic. Subjects range from writing business plans to technology issues.

Bplans.com

`www.bplans.com`

> You need a business plan before you can get financing for your new business—not to mention the need to clarify your plans and prospects before starting. Learn by example at Bplans.com by searching for sample plans that best match your business type (free registration is required). Interactive tools walk you through calculating starting costs, finding financing options, creating an initial assessment for your business plan, and more. Although this site's goal is to sell business-planning software and other products, a number of the resources here are free to all.

Business Owners' Idea Cafe

www.businessownersideacafe.com

> Take a break with the flavorful business fare at the Business Owners' Idea Cafe—"A Fun Approach to Serious Business." Free registration gains you access to the small business grant center, newsletter, contests, opportunities to promote your business, and more. Interact with other entrepreneurs and experts in the Cyberschmooz area, find tons of resources for starting and running a small business, and relax in specialized sections for Generation X and work-at-home moms. Although the approach might be casual, the advice is anything but. You'll find a lot of useful information in a quick and friendly format.

CCH Business Owner's Toolkit

www.toolkit.cch.com

> This site bills itself as "Total know-how for small business." It offers a great deal of useful information and tools to let you start and run your own successful business. Scroll down to see the different categories in the small business guide, ranging from writing a business plan to hiring the right people. You'll also find free downloadable business tools, including sample policies and forms that you can use and/or modify for your own purposes. One interesting feature is free e-mail-based HR training courses for small business owners. Also check out the Ask Alice! advice column for Q&A on small business issues.

EntreWorld

www.entreworld.org

> This ad-free public-service Web site from the Kauffman Foundation contains more than 1,000 searchable resources for entrepreneurs, divided into information on starting your business, growing your business, and finding support. Monthly feature articles on topics from mentoring to balancing entrepreneurial and family issues provide fresh content to keep you visiting. Sign up for this site's free e-mail newsletter for news, updates, and recommended resources—as well as a reminder of new Web site features. Also

search the calendar of events for small business events and seminars near you.

How to Start a Business

`http://home.inreach.com/sbdc/book/`

An online book and award-winning Web site in one, this site from the San Joaquin Delta College Small Business Development Center is chock-full of information and resources on starting your own business. Start with the table of contents to get a breakdown of the topics covered here, or read straight through for complete coverage of all the steps involved. Each section includes links to additional articles, information, and sites, and an interactive index allows you to locate the specific information you need with just a click.

Network Solutions

`www.netsol.com`

The granddaddy of domain registrars, VeriSign-owned Network Solutions lets you search to see whether your first, second, or fifteenth domain name choice is available, and then register your site name online. You'll also find tips for building traffic and managing your Internet business. Network Solutions is only one of many domain name registration services. For more (and often cheaper) options, see the Accredited Registrar Directory from ICANN, the Internet Corporation for Assigned Names and Numbers, at www.internic.net/regist.html.

Nolo.com

`www.nolo.com`

Nolo prides itself on "putting the law into plain English"—just the ticket for a busy small business owner! Most of what you need can be found in the Small Business section, which includes articles, FAQs, and advice on issues from small business legal structures to accounting. You can also locate and purchase helpful do-it-yourself legal titles and software from Nolo if you need further information or print references. Get information to help yourself or to be an informed customer when dealing with your attorney.

OPEN Small Business Network from American Express

`www.americanexpress.com/homepage/smallbusiness.shtml`

> American Express of course wants you to sign up to use its card in your small business, but it provides a great deal of free information and articles along the way. Check out the online question-and-answer forums, where you can connect with other small business owners, or ask your question of the small business advisor to receive expert advice. Online quizzes gauge your entrepreneurial aptitude, workshops walk you through tasks such as writing a business plan, and articles highlight common issues facing small business owners.

Yahoo! Small Business

`http://smallbusiness.yahoo.com`

> Yahoo! Small Business does what Yahoo! does best: categorize sites and articles for your browsing pleasure. Choose from Solutions, Resources, Technology, Articles, and Marketplace and then drill down further to specific topics of interest. A number of links here are sponsored, so research your options carefully before buying anything from one of these sites.

Franchises

Franchises provide a ready-made business opportunity for those who want to start their own business with the security of an established brand behind their efforts. The sites in this section cover places to find franchise opportunities and franchising in general.

BISON: The Franchise Network

`www.bison1.com`

> Thinking of buying a franchise? BISON can help steer your efforts. Search here for franchise opportunities by subject, and find information on each company, including costs. Each includes a link to request more information. Learn more about the franchising

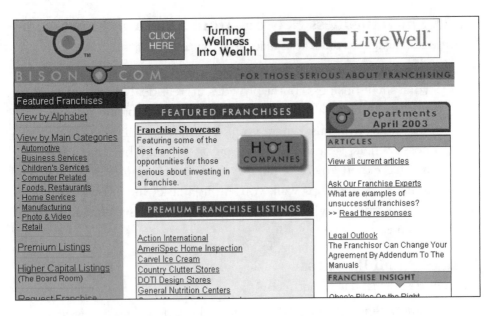

process and get tips for success by reading feature articles, or ask the experts your franchising question. You'll also find franchising news, profiles of featured franchises, and financing options.

Entrepreneur.com Franchise Zone

`www.entrepreneur.com/Franchise_Zone/`

On this portal for franchisers, you'll find news, advice, articles, and assistance. The franchise directory contains categorized opportunities. The information on each company includes investment requirements, fees, and funding information; background and contact info; information on franchise growth; the type of training and support the company provides; and suggestions of where it is seeking franchisees. Also check out the Franchise 500 for hot opportunities as well as lists of home-based, low-investment, fastest-growing, and other types of franchises. Check out the link to *Franchise Zone* magazine for articles, tips, and how-tos.

Franchise UPDATE

`http://franchise-update.com`

This self-proclaimed "ultimate resource for franchise opportunities" certainly contains a wealth of them! Check the Franchise Live directory for opportunities that you can browse alphabetically or by category, geographic location, investment level, and so on. Each result gives basic information on the franchise, including contact information and investment requirements and a form for requesting further info. Also check out the link to Franchisor Update, a site containing news, events, and other information for franchise executives.

Online Business Magazines

Many online business magazines take full advantage of the Web to provide fast-breaking and current content to business owners and entrepreneurs. Web content provides added value to print subscribers and nonsubscribers alike.

Business 2.0

www.business2.com

> Business 2.0 is the source of business information in the Internet era. Its focus is on how the Internet and changing technologies affect business, although much of the advice and insights here apply to any company. Start with the Web Guide, a compendium of handpicked links to the best business resources on the Web, and then read monthly feature articles and daily news stories to keep up with how you and your business can deal with change. Other features include free e-mail newsletters and sponsored panel discussions held in various locations across the country.

Entrepreneur.com

www.entrepreneur.com

> This searchable companion site to several magazines for entrepreneurs and small business owners contains much more than articles. Start by signing up for free topical e-mail newsletters on topics such as starting a business, growing a business, and e-business. The Small-Biz Essentials section contains articles, tips, expert advice, and more in areas ranging from home-based businesses to

sales and marketing. The Franchise Zone provides searchable listings and information on the fastest-growing franchises. Read about
technology, management, e-business—the list is nearly endless.
This site is worthy of multiple visits.

Fast Company

www.fastcompany.com

Fast Company concentrates on dealing with change, but because it
focuses much more than Business 2.0 on free agency, "brand you,"
and community, much of the content is more applicable to individuals and small business owners. Sign up for free e-mail newsletters, participate in online forums, or access any article through
subject-separated online guides. Also find profiles of interesting
and innovative companies and use them to glean ideas for growing your own business.

Fortune Small Business

www.fortune.com/smallbusiness/

This online counterpart to the magazine of the same name features
selected articles from the print issue (with added Web-only
features), online-only articles, advice, a free e-mail newsletter, and

more. Start with the categorized Best Web Sites for Entrepreneurs to spark your own ideas, and then check out the calendar for small business events near you. Other useful content includes profiles of successful companies, focusing on how they got started. You can learn by example!

Inc.com

www.inc.com

Inc.com guides contain the best handpicked resources for small business—and Inc. has been doing this a long time. Read the current issue, browse through the archives, search for articles of interest, or browse by subject. How-to guides and free e-mail newsletters will keep you reading, and online forums let you interact with others. Join for free to access useful tools such as sample business letters, worksheets, and agreements.

Business Associations

Business associations are a great place to network with other small business owners, get ideas, find resources, and build new business opportunities. This section contains some Web sites of general associations to get you started. You should also look for associations focusing on your business's specialty.

National Association for the Self-Employed (NASE)

www.nase.org

Self-employed individuals face particular issues, from finding affordable health coverage to financing a small business. NASE aims to help members tackle such issues through providing information, member benefits, and lobbying for small business interests. Member benefits here range from health insurance breaks to savings on common services such as shipping and business phone service. Join to add your voice and be an advocate for your own interests—or simply for the benefits! Other site features include news, advice, and reference materials.

National Federation of Independent Business (NFIB)

www.nfib.com

> Another advocacy organization for small business, NFIB's more than 600,000 members have a significant voice. Learn about state and national issues facing small business owners, read useful articles, and find out about member benefits here. Member benefits are similar to NASE, including health, travel, service, and other discounts. Research each carefully to see which association is right for you.

U.S. Chamber of Commerce

www.uschamber.com

> One of your first steps upon establishing your small business should be to join your local Chamber of Commerce. For a minimal yearly fee, Chambers provide invaluable networking opportunities, business contacts, and business education for local business owners. Use the Chamber Directory at this site to locate yours and to link directly to its Web site (when available) for more information. The U.S. Chamber of Commerce site also includes news, events, member benefits, and advocacy information, so explore this site as well as your local Chamber.

SOHO: Small Office/Home Office

More than 20 million Americans now work at least one day a week from home, either through a telecommuting/freelance arrangement with outside employers or in their own home-based business. The U.S. Department of Labor predicts that half of all Americans will be working at least partially from home by 2025. The work-at-home trend continues so strongly that it's become a market segment with its own catchy acronym: SOHO (small office/home office). The Web sites in this section cover the SOHO phenomenon. For information on telecommuting, contracting, and freelancing, see chapter 9.

Business@Home

www.gohome.com

> Business@Home is an e-zine with a simple motto: "Making a life while making a living." This site is set up like a typical magazine, with feature stories and departments as well as regularly updated sections showcasing articles on legal issues, SOHO technology, marketing, and more.

Home Office Association of America

www.hoaa.com

> Here you learn about the membership benefits of the Home Office Association of America. These include a biweekly e-mail newsletter, group savings on health insurance, low-cost long-distance service, home business and equipment insurance, and merchant credit card services. Also check out the Startups section for a number of business ideas.

The ParentPreneur Club

www.parentpreneurclub.com

> The ParentPreneur Club is sponsored by NOBOSS, a catchy acronym that stands for the National Organization of Business Opportunity Seekers. Read articles aimed at parents who have (or want to have) a home-based business, view online tutorials, and browse the links list for a ton of other work-at-home resources.

You can also sign up for free membership to get two newsletters and other members-only benefits, such as access to a database of business opportunities that can be launched with $50 to $5,000 of initial investment. Be sure to take the time to interact with other entrepreneurial parents in the online forums.

Small Business Advisor

www.isquare.com

Plenty of current information is available at Small Business Advisor. Want FAQs? They're here. Small business advice and articles? Of course. You'll also find daily and weekly tips on advertising, marketing, accounting, taxes, stress, and other issues facing small business owners. Sign up for a free monthly e-mail newsletter or read a weekly free Web-based newsletter. Locate information for small businesses in your state. Start with the advice for first-time visitors to learn how to optimize your time at this site—there's a lot to wade through!

Working from Home (Paul and Sarah Edwards)

www.homeworks.com

The authors of several best-selling books on self-employment, Paul and Sarah Edwards provide a number of excerpts and extras for Web site visitors. Online quizzes, suggestions, sample chapters, FAQs, articles, newsletters, special reports, and more can spur you on your way to following your dream of working for yourself, doing work you love. Daily tips and special reports provide concrete suggestions for existing home-based businesses. This site is sure to inspire those aspiring to self-employment.

Working Solo

www.workingsolo.com

When you're trying to make it on your own, you often feel like you need a helping hand. Working Solo extends that hand by providing a free quarterly e-mail newsletter, FAQs about starting a solo business, and SOHO resources and articles. You also get a handy outline of the current state of SOHO businesses in the U.S. This Web site is the companion to the *Working Solo* series of books by best-selling SOHO author Terri Lonier.

Resources for Women Business Owners

SBA and SBA-Sponsored Resources

Office of Women's Business Ownership (SBA)

www.sbaonline.sba.gov/womeninbusiness

Here you'll learn about the special services the SBA provides women business owners, in addition to the Online Women's Business Center (discussed next). This Web site has up-to-date contact information for local Women's Business Centers and Women's Business Ownership representatives. It also sponsors WNET (Women's Network for Entrepreneurial Training), which matches successful mentors with women business owners ready to take the next step to grow their company. Read the monthly success story for inspiration in your own small business efforts and then research lending programs and other services to help women succeed in business.

Online Women's Business Center (OWBC)

www.onlinewbc.gov

There are more than 9 million woman-owned businesses in the U.S., and the SBA Office of Women's Business Ownership-sponsored OWBC aims to help them (and newer startups) succeed. Scroll down to start with answers to FAQs such as "How do I finance my business?" and "Is there help for women with special needs?" The site also contains an extensive list of links to women's business organizations, standard information on starting, running, and growing a business, and information on local Women's Business Centers. Can't find what you're looking for? Search or try the A–Z Index. Much of the site is also available in Spanish, Russian, Japanese, and other languages.

Other Resources Mainly for Women

National Association of Women Business Owners (NAWBO)

www.nawbo.org

Although most of the content at this Web site is accessible only to members, you can also explore as a guest to see what NAWBO offers women entrepreneurs. Like the business associations discussed earlier in this chapter, NAWBO provides member benefits such as corporate and insurance discounts. Members' profiles are also entered in a Web directory, for easy networking with other women business owners. News, articles, discussion boards, and legislative updates provide added value, as does the availability of a number of local chapters.

WAHM.com: Work at Home Moms

www.wahm.com

WAHM.com, the online magazine for work-at-home-moms (WAHMs), provides a ton of resources in a friendly format to appeal to busy moms. These include a free weekly e-mail newsletter, telecommuting job listings, online forums, work-at-home ideas, business opportunities, a directory of WAHMs near you—and more! Promote your business by adding information to the online WAHM directory, and don't forget to enjoy the weekly cartoon.

WomanOwned.com

www.womanowned.com

Here you can use the online search engine of women business owners to find and network with other woman-owned businesses and continue your networking efforts in their online forums. Free basic membership gives you access to discounts on health insurance and other services, a monthly newsletter, affiliate program access, and more. Advanced (paid) membership provides additional benefits. Informational sections cover starting a business, getting money, writing a business plan, adding employees, government contracting, marketing and sales, certification, growing your business, and using the Web for sales. Each category contains a useful overview and links for further information.

Welcome to **WAHM**™**.com**
The Online Magazine for Work at Home Moms℠

Click on me if this is your first
time here and I'll show you around.

Is every day *"Take our children to work"* day?
Are there Legos under your desk?
Is your coffeepot the most-used appliance in your house?
Then you're a WAHM, and this is your magazine!

YOU KNOW YOUR VEHICLE IS TOO BIG WHEN YOU
NEED A WALKIE-TALKIE TO HEAR YOUR KIDS

"MOM! I NEED A
BATHROOM
BREAK!
-OVER-"

My new book!
Coming this May from Warner Books,
But you can pre-order it now, just
click here:

It's a Jungle Out There
and a Zoo in Here

CHAPTER 9

Temporary, Freelance, Telecommuting, and Volunteer Work

Another way to get started in a great career is to investigate "alternative" opportunities as a temporary worker, freelancer, telecommuter, or volunteer. These include full- and part-time opportunities in your own home, in your community, or around the world. Although some pay well and others don't pay at all, each provides valuable experience and can open your eyes to careers you might not have thought of.

Flex Work

Flex work options include part- and full-time temporary, contract, and freelance or free-agent work.

Temp Work, Flex Work, and Contract Employment

If you're always up for new challenges and enjoy variety in your life, temp work might be for you! There is always high demand for skilled temps, and companies that have downsized have created a whole new market for temp and contract employees to fill in the gaps. Temps and contractors generally work for and are paid by an agency that places them in various settings. Although hourly wages might be somewhat higher, you often have to balance this against a lack of employer-sponsored bene-fits, but temping lets you get your foot in the door and can often lead to permanent employment.

The Contract Employee's Handbook

www.cehandbook.com

> Contract employees, sometimes called leased employees, are employed by a contract employment agency and are assigned to work in client companies. Here you'll find out how to deal with employment agencies, set your rates, and create a great contractor resume, and you can browse a ton of links to other resources, both on- and offline. You also can sign up for a free biweekly e-mail newsletter for professional and technical contractors. (You need the free Adobe Acrobat Reader from www.adobe.com to take full advantage of this site.)

Kelly Services

www.kellyservices.us

> Kelly Services, the big name in temp agencies, provides employees in a variety of fields to companies around the globe. Search for contract and regular opportunities by location, category, or key-word, or register as a "preferred candidate" to have jobs meeting your personal criteria e-mailed to you daily and to post your resume online. Check out Kelly's "employment tools" for salary surveys, career assessment tools, articles, and more.

Manpower Inc.

www.manpower.com

> One of the biggest providers of staffing services worldwide, Manpower provides a searchable database of current opportunities, a list of local offices, and information on why you might want to work for Manpower. You might also want to check out the Global Learning Center, which provides free online training opportunities for Manpower employees.

Monster: Contract and Temporary

http://ct.monster.com

> The main attraction of this site is its database of searchable temporary and contract positions. You can see what's available from a number of agencies and companies rather than working with just one staffing agency. Also check out career advice and resources targeted at temporary and contract workers, as well as an online message board for contractors.

Net-Temps

`www.net-temps.com`

Net-Temps specializes in job postings for the staffing industry, including both contract and direct-hire positions. You can search the job listings by keyword or browse by category. You can also register to post your resume online (from Microsoft Word or using the resume builder tool), use job search agents, and receive postings via e-mail. When searching, specify whether you would like just contract positions or both contract and direct-hire opportunities. You can apply online for most positions, and quick apply lets you paste your resume into a form for easy sending to employers. You can also read a number of career development articles and get advice on changing careers.

Freelancers, Free Agents, E-Lancers, and Independent Professionals

When you think of freelancers, most likely professions such as writing and photography come to mind. But here, as everywhere else, new opportunities are opening up for people with all types of talents. Whether you call yourself a freelancer or a consultant, companies are finding more and more uses for skilled outside professionals. Use the sites in this section to "hire your own employer."

All Freelance Work

`www.allfreelancework.com`

Post your profile or distribute your resume to recruiters for a small fee, or conduct a free meta-search of 15 freelance job sites. Free registration gives you access to All Freelance Work's own job search, and you can also connect with other independent contractors through online forums and read or contribute articles on the freelancing life.

Aquent

www.aquent.com

Aquent works like an agent for creative and IT professionals, helping them find projects, temp work, and full-time employment. Fill out an online application to see whether Aquent will represent you. If you are hired through Aquent, it handles billing and the other details involved in contract work.

Creative Freelancers

www.freelancers.com

Freelance designers, illustrators, writers, editors, photographers, Web designers, and other creative types can get Internet exposure through Creative Freelancers. Enter your free profile into the database and show up in talent searches conducted by both Creative Freelancers and outside employers. Value-added information includes a pricing guide, legal help, and links to clubs, organizations, and other resources for creative professionals.

Elance.com

www.elance.com

Companies or individuals post project proposals open for your bid, or you can post your own fixed-price service listing. Formerly free, Elance is now a subscription-only site. Choose the monthly, quarterly, or yearly option, or subscribe by category to see only listings appropriate to your industry. Extensive tips guide you through the process, and sample letters and agreements are available for free.

Free Agent Nation

www.freeagentnation.com

A companion Web site to the book of the same name, Free Agent Nation includes extensive news articles and information on everything from health insurance to tax information to career advice for free agents. Connect with others through free agent clubs, and sign up for a free e-mail newsletter. This refreshingly noncommercial site estimates that about one in four Americans is a free agent. The advice and information here can help you join their ranks.

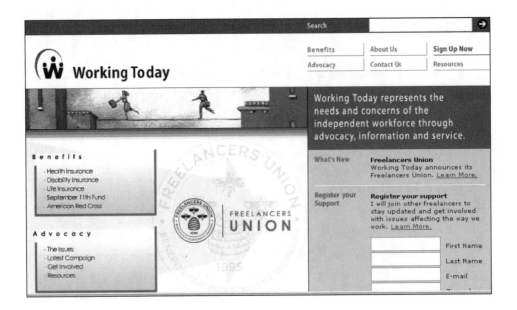

Working Today

`www.workingtoday.org`

New York-based freelancers and contractors will especially appreciate Working Today's group-rate health plan offer, and the organization is currently working to expand benefits to other cities. Join for a minimal yearly fee to receive member discounts on legal and dental services, office products, and other items useful to independent workers. Browse through helpful resources and articles for further information on topics such as benefit issues and finances.

Teleworking/Telecommuting

In 2001, nearly 30 million Americans worked at least one day a week at home or otherwise away from a conventional office. The events of September 11 only added to the push for more-flexible working arrangements. Phone, fax, e-mail, and online services allow telecommuters to keep in constant contact with their home office. Most report increased job satisfaction, productivity, and employer loyalty. Challenges exist, however, including that of managing your time effectively and losing out on the in-person companionship of work colleagues. Realize that many employers do not advertise positions as telecommuting. Often this is an arrangement you make with your employer after you have worked for some time on-site. This section has some resources for telecommuting or teleworking jobs and information. Also see the "SOHO: Small Office/Home Office" and "Resources for Women Business Owners" sections in chapter 8 for more on working from home.

Better Business Bureau: Work-At-Home Schemes

www.bbb.org/library/workathome.asp

> A number of unscrupulous individuals and companies have taken advantage of people's desire to work from home and the power of the Internet to perpetrate work-at-home scams on job seekers. The Better Business Bureau here provides information on how to avoid being taken, including a list of the most common scams with sample job ads to avoid. Also find out who you can contact if you are victimized by one of these schemes. The best advice? If it sounds too good to be true, it probably is!

HomeWorkersNet

www.homeworkersnet.com

> Your first step here is to sign up for the free e-mail newsletter that lists work-at-home job opportunities. Then go on to explore the rest of the site, including a job listings section that pulls work-at-home opportunities from a number of job banks. Each opening is researched by HomeWorkersNet to help you avoid less-than-legitimate offers. Check back often for daily featured

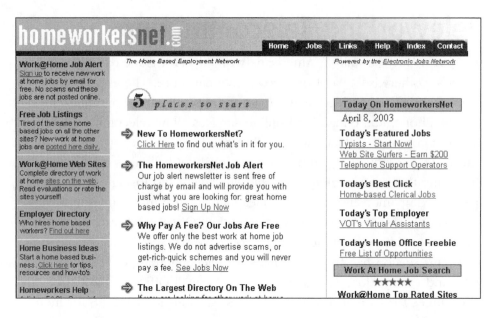

positions. Other sections include a directory of other sites devoted to home-based employment, an employer directory, home business ideas, and articles and advice. It's a great place to start for anyone interested in working from home.

InnoVisions Canada/Canadian Telework Association

`www.ivc.ca`

Telework/flexwork consultants InnoVisions Canada and the non-profit Canadian Telework Association team up here to provide a ton of worldwide information, statistics, and resources on telecommuting. Find out about everything from telecommuting and disabilities to conferences to taxes—and anything in between.

International Telework Association and Council

`www.workingfromanywhere.org`

Join the International Telework Association and Council (ITAC) to get access to research reports and discounts on products and services, or just browse through the free information on this site for conference dates, articles, quick facts, links, and online "webinars" on telecommuting topics.

PortaJobs

www.portajobs.com

> Free registration allows you to access employer contact information and receive e-mail notifications of new postings matching your online profile. You can choose to keep your contact information confidential while having your resume and "skills profile" remain searchable by employers. Access reports and news to find out more about telecommuting trends.

Telecommuting Jobs

www.tjobs.com

> View and respond to free job listings in categories including artists, programmers, writers, Web designers, data entry, and engineers. Create a low-cost "InSiteOffice" page that shows you have the at-home setup to accomplish certain tasks, and post your resume online to show up in talent searches by employers. Other helpful sections include free articles and statistics, as well as links to certification, training, and other useful resources for telecommuters.

YouCanWorkFromAnywhere.com

www.youcanworkfromanywhere.com

> Telecommuters, mobile workers, "road warriors," and home-based workers can find tips, articles, classes, e-books, newsletters, and more on working effectively in nontraditional ways. Find out how to avoid work-at-home scams, how to use technology effectively while telecommuting, and where to find telecommuting job listings online. This comprehensive site is a great place to find information on getting started as a telecommuter and working more effectively from home.

Volunteer Opportunities

Volunteering, of course, means offering your services for no pay. But given that volunteering gives you valuable experience for your resume—and the intangible benefits of being able to make a difference in the world—you might consider adding a volunteer stint to your career plans. You'll find "job banks" of volunteer opportunities and virtual volunteer positions, because the Internet has made it easier to match volunteers with organizations needing their help. If you find that making a difference through your work is important to you, many of these sites also list job opportunities with nonprofit organizations. Volunteering also gives you experience you can later translate into paid work.

4 Labors of Love

www.4laborsoflove.org

/ Here you can register and post your skills online so that nonprofit organizations can contact you for internships or volunteer opportunities, or search through listings posted online. As with Internet job banks, you can register to be alerted via e-mail when new opportunities matching your skills and interests become available.

American Red Cross

www.redcross.org/services/volunteer/

/ Want to help out, but the thought of giving blood makes you squeamish? Volunteers comprise 97% of the Red Cross's workforce, so check the American Red Cross's volunteer recruitment Web site for other opportunities. Read all about the organization's disaster relief, health and safety courses, and other services, including inspirational stories from volunteers and thank-you letters from communities. Search volunteer opportunities by zip code, category, and date, or get contact information for the American Red Cross chapter nearest you.

Corporation for National and Community Service

www.cns.gov

This federally funded site offers three major opportunities for public service. Through Americorps, volunteers devote a year to giving back to the community through educational, environmental, health, and public safety services. Senior Corps taps the skills of older citizens through foster grandparents, senior companions, and other volunteer opportunities. Service-Learning lets America's younger generation combine volunteerism with education through their schools. Find out about these programs, search for other volunteer opportunities, or connect with other members or service alums.

Idealist

www.idealist.org

Idealist brings together nonprofit organizations and volunteers with a searchable database of opportunities. Sign up to have new opportunities e-mailed to you and to have your skills listed in the database so that organizations can easily find you. Other neat ideas here include volunteering with your family, volunteering abroad, and making a career out of nonprofit work by searching Idealist's career center for jobs and internships with these organizations. You can also search for or browse organizations by area of interest or geographic location to find out who is doing what.

NetAid

www.netaid.org/ov/

Here's a new idea: Volunteer your skills online to help organizations make a difference in the developing world—without leaving home! Just some of the areas of expertise needed are translation services, Web site creation, writing, researching, programming, and offering expert advice. This is the perfect opportunity to volunteer your skills while holding down a day job. Search through available assignments online, find out about projects, and fill out online applications to contact organizations and offer your skills.

Network for Good

www.network4good.com

Network for Good uses the power of the Web to help people get more involved in their communities. The Volunteer section features searchable volunteer opportunities, including one-time events, ongoing programs, full-time service, volunteer networks, international opportunities, and virtual opportunities. Also check out the articles on volunteering and links to Web sites where you can find additional opportunities.

Peace Corps

www.peacecorps.gov

Here you can find out about recruiting events, e-mail or find a recruiter, or apply online to serve overseas as a Peace Corps volunteer. The Peace Corps needs volunteers in areas such as education, information technology, agriculture, health, environment, business, and community development. Read through stories from volunteers to find out what volunteering abroad is really like, read news stories, and find out about other benefits such as student loan deferment, job placement, and training services for returned volunteers.

Points of Light Foundation

`www.pointsoflight.org`

/ This site helps you locate your local Points of Light volunteer center, find out about the foundation and its mission, and get ideas for ways you can help in your everyday life. Points of Light also sponsors special volunteer days and community efforts, so you can find out about upcoming events on this site. Also find out how to answer the president's "call to service" by searching through volunteer opportunities by area of interest and geographic location.

SERVEnet

`www.servenet.org`

/ SERVEnet is a free matching service for volunteers and organizations. Either do a quick search by zip code to list organizations and opportunities in your area, or use the advanced search to more closely match your skills to available opportunities. You can also find out about special volunteer events across the nation, virtual (online) volunteer opportunities, and how to be a successful volunteer. You also can browse job openings with nonprofit organizations.

Teach For America

`www.teachforamerica.org`

/ Are you a recent college graduate with a desire to teach? Do you have a sense of adventure? Do you want to make a difference? Each year, this public-service program conducts summer training institutes for qualified recent graduates who have degrees in any subject. Teach For America then places nearly 2,000 trained corps members as full-time, paid teachers in schools with critical needs. Subscribe to the free applicant newsletter, fill out an online application, and find out more about the program at this Web site.

United Nations Volunteers

`www.unv.org`

/ Unlike Teach For America, United Nations Volunteers specifically seeks mid-career applicants who are interested in putting their skills to use worldwide. Each year, about 5,000 volunteers from more than 150 countries contribute their efforts to this program, which works through United Nations Development Programme offices around the world. Find out how to apply to volunteer at home, abroad, or online, and sign up to be included in the skills bank of interested candidates.

VolunteerMatch

`www.volunteermatch.org`

VolunteerMatch provides a free matching service for volunteers and organizations. Put in your zip code to find places to volunteer in your area, or choose the "virtual" volunteering option and browse through ways to contribute your skills without leaving your house. This Web site also lets you create a personal volunteer account to receive personalized e-mails and manage your online volunteer resume.

Volunteer-Related Associations

If you're interested in a professional career either with a nonprofit or in the field of volunteerism, you might want to investigate what these associations have to offer.

Alliance for Nonprofit Management

`www.allianceonline.org`

The Alliance for Nonprofit Management is devoted to the management and government of nonprofit organizations. Its new Alliance Resource Center includes hundreds of books, sites, videos, programs, organizations, and newsletters in every area of nonprofit management, which you can browse by area of interest. This Web site also includes an online CareerBank, which can be searched by location and position type, as well as a free online newsletter.

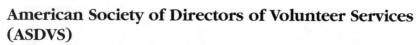

American Society of Directors of Volunteer Services (ASDVS)

www.hospitalconnect.com/DesktopServlet

Hospitals are a major employer of volunteers, and the American Society of Directors of Volunteer Services is the only national professional organization for directors of volunteer services in health care. Here you can learn about ways to manage health-care volunteers effectively, browse news and events, and find out about conferences and educational opportunities. You can become a member of the site to receive special member benefits. This Web site also includes a browsable list of volunteer opportunities.

Association for Volunteer Administration (AVA)

www.avaintl.org

AVA, a professional association for leaders/managers of volunteers, provides an online job bank, links to educational opportunities in the field, and information on its credentialing program for managers of volunteers. Network with others in your field through the e-mail discussion list for volunteer management professionals or by finding a local professional association near you.

Association of Fundraising Professionals

www.nsfre.org

Fundraising requires a special set of skills. If you have these skills and want to put them to good use in a career helping a nonprofit organization raise badly needed funds, this is the organization for you. This Web site provides information on how the organization promotes charitable giving and on how you can develop your career and education as a fundraising professional. Register with the site to apply for jobs listed in its online service.

National Council of Nonprofit Associations (NCNA)

`www.ncna.org`

NCNA is a network of 37 state and regional nonprofit associations representing more than 21,000 nonprofits. Its mission includes raising the profile of nonprofits and providing them with the tools and leadership they need to function more effectively. Find out about current projects, browse job openings with member associations and partners, and find out about events in your area.

Glossary

ACT (American College Testing Assessment)   A standardized college admissions test measuring a student's scholastic development. Most colleges base admissions decisions on a combination of grades, activities, and scores on standardized tests such as this or the SAT.

address book   In your e-mail client software, the list of nicknames and addresses of people to whom you frequently send messages.

affiliate program   An agreement between Web-based businesses to direct viewers to other Web sites through links, usually with a commission for resulting sales.

apprenticeship   A job-training program that combines classroom training with on-the-job training.

autoresponder   An e-mail software feature that automatically sends a response to each incoming e-mail message.

BLS (U.S. Department of Labor Bureau of Labor Statistics)   The primary federal source of data on employment.

bookmarks   In Netscape Navigator, a way to save the addresses of your favorite Web sites so that you can return to them easily in the future. The same feature is called "Favorites" in Microsoft Internet Explorer.

Boolean logic   The form of logic used by many search engines that allows you to control how narrow or broad a search you want to conduct by combining search terms in certain ways. Named for mathematician George Boole.

bot   Short for "robot." A software tool sent out by a search engine to dig through the Web for your requested information.

browser   A program used to view Web pages. The most well-known browser programs are Microsoft Internet Explorer and Netscape Navigator. You also might encounter other browsers, such as Mozilla and Opera.

bulletin board   See *forum.*

career information   Descriptions of careers that might include attributes such as job requirements, skills, educational preparation, working conditions, employment outlook, and wages.

chat   To communicate online in real time. The person with whom you are chatting can see your words as you type them or immediately after you press Enter. Also called *instant messaging* or *IM.*

clearinghouse   A Web site that contains lists of other Web sites, organized by related topics.

continuing education   Courses available to adults who are not enrolled in a formal degree program. Also, education undertaken after you complete a degree program to remain current in your field, sometimes required for maintaining licensure or certification. Continuing-education credits may be awarded for courses, workshops, or conferences.

contracting   Providing specific services to a company for a specified period of time, for a specified payment.

cover letter   A letter written to accompany a resume. It expresses your interest in the position you are applying for and gives an overview of your skills.

database   An organized collection of data that you can access and sort by selected criteria. For example, a job bank is an online database of available jobs. You could direct it to sort only the jobs in your state, as opposed to those across the country.

demographics   Data about the age, race, sex, income, and other details of people living in a certain area. Applications of demographic data include targeting advertising or getting an idea of the labor market in a particular area.

dial-up access   A way to connect to the Internet over standard telephone lines. Most home Internet connections are still dial-up accounts.

Dictionary of Occupational Titles (DOT)   A reference publication, based on U.S. Department of Labor data, that classifies and briefly describes more than 12,000 jobs.

directory   A place on a computer or server where data files are stored. Directories are used to separate files into related groups and specify the location of the files on the computer.

distance learning   The ability to further your education, either toward a degree or as part of your lifelong learning, by taking courses through learning technologies other than a traditional classroom. These technologies include audiotapes, videotapes, teleconferencing, videoconferencing, and computer-based and Internet-based training.

DOL (U.S. Department of Labor)   The federal agency that oversees all federally funded labor-related programs.

domain   The part of your e-mail address that specifies the name of the ISP through which you access your e-mail, such as aol.com. Also, the part of a Web address that identifies the presence of a company or organization on the Internet.

download   To copy files from the Internet to your computer's hard drive.

e-lancer   A self-employed individual who contracts for work primarily through the Internet.

electronic resume   Any resume in a computerized format, usually in Microsoft Word, ASCII text, HTML, or PDF.

e-mail   Electronic mail. A written message sent from one person's online address to another's via the Internet or another computer network.

e-mail discussion list   An e-mail group in which a message posted by any member is disseminated to all members of the group, any of whom are free to respond and participate in the discussion.

emoticons   Pictures in e-mail that are composed of keyboard characters indicating the mood of the person writing the message. For example, :) indicates a smiling face.

ETA (U.S. Department of Labor Employment and Training Administration)   The federal agency responsible for federally funded employment and training programs.

FAQ (Frequently Asked Questions)   A list of answers to the questions that Web site visitors are likely to ask repeatedly.

Favorites   In Internet Explorer, a way to save the addresses of your favorite Web sites so that you can return to them easily in the future. The same feature is called "bookmarks" in Netscape Navigator.

file name   The name of the document that contains the data on a Web page. Many Web page file names end with the letters .htm or .html.

financial aid   The combination of scholarships, grants, and loans that a student uses to pay for college. Financial aid is limited to the amount of actual "need" that is determined for the student.

flex work   Nontraditional work arrangements such as contracting, freelancing, and temporary work.

forum   An online discussion group. Sometimes called a *bulletin board.*

franchise   A business in which you buy the right to use the name and the established procedures and products in exchange for a percentage of the profits.

free agent   A self-employed individual who works on a contract basis, often for more than one employer.

freelancer   A self-employed individual who works on a contract basis, often for more than one employer.

freeware   Software (such as games and utilities) that you can download from the Internet and use for free.

FTP (File Transfer Protocol)   A protocol for transferring files from one computer to another over the Internet.

graphical user interface (GUI)   The graphical menus, tools, and buttons you see on-screen, which help you work with a particular program using the mouse's point-and-click features.

GRE (Graduate Record Exam)   The test taken by college seniors for admission to graduate programs.

guaranty agency   The state agency or private, nonprofit organization that administers federally funded student loans.

home page   A Web site's initial page or starting page. Also, the page you set to appear when you first open your browser or click the Home button.

host   Any computer on a network that is a repository for services available to other computers on the network.

HTML (Hypertext Markup Language)   The coding that is used to turn regular text into a Web page that can be viewed by a browser.

hyperlink (link)   An (often highlighted) word, phrase, or graphic on a Web page that is connected to another Internet document. By clicking it, you are taken to a related Web page, either on the same site or on a completely different Web site.

hypertext   Text that contains one or more hyperlinks.

independent professional A self-employed individual who works on a contract basis, often for more than one employer.

indexed search engines Search engines, such as AltaVista, that locate Web pages based on text found on the page or keywords in meta-tags hidden in a document's coding.

infrastructure The essential, underlying elements of an entity or organization that allow it to function.

instant messaging See *chat*.

Internet directory Reviews and organizes the information on the Web into categories. Each broad category, such as "Business & Economy," has more specific categories under it, and those categories have even more specific categories under them. Yahoo! is an example of an Internet directory.

Internet Explorer Microsoft's Internet browser program, used to view and move between Web pages. Internet Explorer is built into Microsoft Windows.

Internet Service Provider (ISP) A national or local company that, for a monthly fee, lets you connect to the Internet. Examples of national ISPs include America Online, AT&T WorldNet, and Earthlink.

internship A program in which a student works for an employer for a specified period of time to learn about a particular occupation. The intern is sometimes paid for the work in addition to receiving college credit.

interview To meet with a potential employer that has a job opening to determine whether you are the right person for the job. In an informational interview, you meet with a person who works in the field in which you are interested so that you can learn about the job and what you need to do to prepare for it.

job bank A Web database of job openings. You can search for specific jobs by title, category, and geographic location, among other variables.

Job Corps A federally funded residential education and job-training program for at-risk youth ages 16 to 24.

job fair A meeting at which employers set up booths and speak with job seekers in an effort to recruit employees.

keyword A word you type into a search engine or Web site search function to help locate information you are seeking.

labor market The pool of both employed and unemployed persons who are currently available and willing to work; the source of applicants for a job opening.

labor market information Data about workers, jobs, industries, and employers, generally used by program planners, analysts, administrators, researchers, employers, and job seekers.

leased employee Someone who works for a company that sells his or her services to another company for a specified period of time. The leasing company (or temporary agency) administers the employee's salaries and benefits. See also *temp*.

link (hyperlink) An (often highlighted) word, phrase, or graphic on a Web page that is connected to another Internet document. By clicking it, you are taken to a related Web page, either on the same site or on a completely different Web site.

listserv™ Trademarked e-mail discussion-management software from the L-soft Corporation, often misused as a generic term for an e-mail discussion list.

load To open a Web page with your browser. The computer temporarily copies the data from the server onto your computer's hard drive.

Macintosh (Mac) A computer introduced by Apple Computer in 1984. The Macintosh was distinguished by its graphical user interface, which allowed users to point and click with a mouse in addition to using a keyboard to operate the system.

mailing list A list of e-mail addresses to which you can send the same e-mail message simultaneously.

message board A place on a Web site where people can post and respond to questions and discussion topics. See also *forum*.

meta-list A list of related Web sites posted on a Web site. Also known as a *clearinghouse*.

meta-search engine A search engine that lets you use several search engines at the same time while entering your search criteria only once.

Microsoft The software company that introduced the Internet Explorer browser program and the Windows operating system, among other programs.

modem The device (either inside or outside your computer) that translates information from your computer and from remote resources into a format that can travel over telephone lines.

multithreaded search engine   See *meta-search engine.*

Netscape   The software company that produced the Netscape Navigator browser program for viewing Web pages.

network   Two or more computers or other devices connected to one another and capable of sharing data. The Internet is a massive, worldwide computer network.

networking   Using your personal contacts to learn about careers and possible job openings.

newsgroup   A topical online discussion group in which you can read and post messages. You can access newsgroups over the Web at http://groups.google.com.

occupational information   Employment data such as wages, anticipated growth, number of people employed, number of new jobs, and other trends.

Occupational Outlook Handbook (OOH)   A reference publication based on U.S. Department of Labor data. It describes the 250 most popular jobs, covering approximately 85 percent of the workforce.

O*NET   The U.S. Department of Labor's electronic database of career and job information on specific occupations.

on-the-job training   Job training that occurs in the workplace.

path   The location of a Web page on a server. It includes the domain name, the directories, and the file name.

plugin   A software program that works with your browser to display added information. Examples of plugins include the Adobe Acrobat Reader and Macromedia Flash.

Portable Document Format (PDF or .pdf)   A file format that allows documents created in any software program and saved in .pdf format to be read through the freely downloadable Adobe Acrobat Reader software. Allows documents to appear and be printed exactly as their creator intended.

Private Industry Council (PIC)   A policy-setting board that administered programs under the federal Job Training Partnership Act for a specific geographic area. Under the Workforce Investment Act, which took effect in 2000, Private Industry Councils became Workforce Investment Boards.

protocol   An agreed-upon format for transferring data from one computer to another.

query To ask a database to sort and show you all the data that meets your specified criteria.

Reserves Military personnel who are not on active duty but who can be called into duty during a war or national crisis.

resume An organized, written summary of your work experience, education, skills, and qualifications. Many job postings request that you submit a resume for consideration.

resume bank A Web site where you can post a copy of your resume for potential employers to view.

robot (bot) A software tool sent out by a search engine to dig through the Web for your requested information.

ROTC (Reserve Officer Training Corps) A cooperative program between colleges and branches of the military that allows undergraduate students to receive officer training while they attend college.

SAT (Scholastic Aptitude Test) A standardized college admissions test. Most colleges base admissions decisions on a combination of grades, activities, and scores on standardized tests such as this.

search engine A Web site that lets you search for other Web sites of interest by entering a keyword or keywords in a search field. Examples of search engines include Google and AltaVista.

self-assessment The process of working to identify, understand, and express your skills, knowledge, abilities, interests, values, personality, motivations, passions, and anything else about you that might affect your career decisions.

server A computer, connected to a network, that manages resources such as files or printers. Web servers contain and serve up Web page documents in response to requests from browsers.

service academy An undergraduate college run by a branch of the armed forces that trains high school graduates to be military officers.

shareware Software that you can download from the Internet and use for a small fee.

signature (e-mail) Information that automatically appears at the bottom of every e-mail you send, specifying such details as your name, your contact information, or your favorite quote. You can change your signature to say whatever you want.

Small Business Administration (SBA) The federal government's primary source of small-business assistance programs under the U.S. Department of Commerce.

software   A computer program that performs a specific task. Examples of software include Internet browsers, word-processing programs, spreadsheets, and games.

SOHO (small office/home office)   An acronym that reflects the growing trend of self-employed persons operating small businesses from inside or outside their home environment.

teleworker (telecommuter, home worker)   An employee who works at least part-time in a home office, communicating with coworkers and clients via telephone, fax, instant messaging, and/or e-mail.

temp   A person who is employed by an agency to fill short-term positions in other companies. This person's salary and benefits are paid by the agency rather than by the companies.

TOEFL (Test of English as a Foreign Language)   Used to determine whether students are ready for mainstream classes with native speakers of English.

traffic (site traffic)   The volume of users who view a particular Web site. Increased traffic helps the owner sell advertising on the site.

upload   To send files from your computer to an Internet location.

URL (Uniform Resource Locator)   A Web site's address, such as http://www.jist.com. The first part (http://) specifies the protocol for the computers to use when transferring data; the second part specifies the computer and domain name of the site you are accessing.

user name   Your unique identifier on a computer system. Many Web sites that ask you to register require you to select a user name. You use this user name and a private password to gain access again later.

Web page   A document located on another computer elsewhere on the Internet that you can view with a browser; one page within a Web site.

Web site   A group of related Web pages, compiled and sponsored by an individual or organization.

Welfare to Work   Federal welfare reform legislation intended to transition welfare recipients to the paid workforce.

Windows   Microsoft's graphical user interface and operating system for IBM-compatible PCs.

workforce   The sector of the population currently employed or that is ready, willing, and able to work.

workforce development   Initiatives and programs addressing the growth and maintenance of an educated, skilled workforce, coordinating with multiple employment and training service providers.

Workforce Investment Act (WIA) of 1998   Federal legislation that replaced the federal Job Training Partnership Act in 2000.

Workforce Investment Board   A policy-setting board that administers programs under the federal Workforce Investment Act, which took effect in 2000.

World Wide Web (WWW or "the Web")   A global network of information that is based on hyperlinks, which let the viewer easily jump from one Web page or Web site to a related page or site.

Index